Somerled

Somerled

HAMMER OF THE NORSE

K M MacPhee
MA; EdB; PhD

NWP
www.nwp.co.uk

NWP is an imprint of
Neil Wilson Publishing Ltd
303 The Pentagon Centre
36 Washington Street
GLASGOW
G3 8AZ

Tel: 0141-221-1117
Fax: 0141-221-5363
E-mail: info@nwp.co.uk
www.nwp.co.uk

A catalogue record for this book is
available from the British Library.

ISBN 1-903238-24-2
Typeset in Garamond
Designed by Mark Blackadder

Printed in Poland

To my parents,
The Reverend and Mrs James Marks

Thig crìoch air an t-saoghal
Ach mairidh gaol is ceòl

Contents

Acknowledgments   IX
List of Maps   XI

PART ONE

The Years Before Somerled

Chapter 1 Scotland, 1100 AD   3
Chapter 2 Kings of Scotland   8
Chapter 3 The Norse Kingdom of Man and the Isles   15
Chapter 4 No Threat From England – Yet!   20
Chapter 5 Viking Terrorists   22
Chapter 6 Celtic Rì   32
Chapter 7 Affairs in Ireland   36
Chapter 8 Lords of Galloway   41
Chapter 9 Dublin Norse   43
Chapter 10 Earls of Orkney   46

PART TWO

The Kingdom of Argyll and the Isles

Chapter 11 Somerled's Ancestry and Claim to Argyll   53
Chapter 12 Rise of Somerled   61
Chapter 13 Building the Kingdom   65
Chapter 14 King of Argyll and Lord of the Isles   73
Chapter 15 Final Campaign   84

PART THREE

The Ships

Glossary of Nautical Terms   92
Chapter 16 Evolution of the Viking Longship   93
Chapter 17 The Gokstad Ship   100
Chapter 18 Viking Ships and their Descendants   109

PART FOUR

The Legacies of Somerled

Chapter 19 Argyll and the Hebrides   119
Chapter 20 Language and Culture   129
Chapter 21 The Rise of the Great Clans   142
Chapter 22 Lords of the Isles   152
Chapter 23 Somhairle's Men   163

Bibliography   *167*
Pronunciation Guide   *171*
Index   *172*

Acknowledgments

I would like to thank all at Neil Wilson Publishing Ltd for their painstaking work in bringing this book to life. In particular I have to thank Neil himself for taking on this project and smoothing its way to completion. Thanks also to editors Morven Dooner and Sallie Moffat, copy-editor Kate Blackadder, book designer Mark Blackadder, cover designer Robbie Porteous and cartographer Don Williams.

At Dunoon, special thanks to Mairead McGillivray and Sallie Condy at the Community Education Centre for humorous and tolerant assistance when the computer became an even bigger mystery to me than usual.

Also, special thanks to my brother, Ronald, for his endless patience and good humour while assisting with proof-reading, for offering useful opinions and for so kindly keeping me company on field trips around the islands and up and down mountains throughout the west coast of Scotland – and for so often gleefully pointing out that what I fondly imagined was a golden eagle in flight above me was, in fact, a crow!

The publisher and I have made every effort to contact all owners of copyright material in this book. Regrettably, in some instances, we were unable to obtain permissions for these, as we could not trace the ownership of the material. In the event that any reader can help NWP in tracing the rightful owners of these sources, they would be extremely grateful if information could be passed directly to them.

I am indebted to the following for permission to reproduce:

Extracts from *The Lands of the Lordship*, Argyll Reproductions Ltd,
    Islay: 5, 130, 133-6
Extracts from IF Grant's *Lordship of the Isles*, Mercat Press,
    Edinburgh: 25, 58, 163
Translation of Bjorn Cripplehand's 'Poem from the Heimskringla',
    Alfred P Smyth, *Warlords and Holy Men*, Edinburgh
    University Press, 1989: 29
Translation of A' Bhirlinn Bharrach, Mr Murdo MacLeod,
    Inverness: 116
Poetry by Kenneth MacKenzie from *The Highland Clearances*
    by John Prebble, published by Martin Secker & Warburg: 137
Extract from James Hunter's *Scottish Highlanders*, Mainstream
    Publishing Co Ltd, Edinburgh: 162
Illustrations from Ian Atkinson, *The Viking Ships*, Cambridge
    University Press, 1979 © Cambridge University Press: 94, 96-9,
    102, 104, 106-7
Illustration by Ole Crumlin-Pedersen © The Viking Ship Museum,
    Denmark: 103
Photographs © University Museum of Cultural Heritage –
    University of Oslo, Norway: 105, 108
Map from Dr David Caldwell, The National Museum of Scotland,
    Edinburgh: 162

List of Maps

1. Ancient North and South Argyll 4
2. The Early Kingdom of the Isles About 950 AD 17
3. Ancient Land Divisions of the Rì 33
4. Ancient Argyll at its Fullest Extent: Loch Broom to the
   Mull of Kintyre 37
5. Irish and Scottish Dalriada 5th – 6th Centuries AD 39
6. Irish Dalriada and Territories Held by Tribes of Gabran,
   Angus, Loarn, Còmghal etc 40
7. Scotland in the Time of Somerled 54
8. Castles in Somerled's Time 63
9. The Situation in 1140: Main Power Blocks 69
10. See of Trondheim (Nidaros) c 1154 77
11. Events of 1153-60 when Somerled Attained the
    Height of His Power 78
12. The Bi-Partite Kingdom of the Isles 1156 81
13. Main Ship Finds Since 1850 94
14. Argyll 118
15. Lewis 131
16. Islay 132
17. Kintyre 136
18. Finlaggan 162

PART ONE

The Years
Before Somerled

CHAPTER ONE

Scotland 1100 AD

'From the wrath of the Vikings, Good Lord, deliver us!'

To the mid-twelfth-century Gaels of the western seaboard of Scotland it must have seemed as if the Good Lord did indeed send someone to deliver them – and that person was Somhairle Mòr MacGhillebhride, future King of Argyll and Lord of the Isles.

He was the most important leader of Gaelic Scotland after King Kenneth MacAlpin, who brought about the union of the Scots and the Picts in the ninth century, thus beginning the long process leading to the final unification of Scotland as a sovereign nation. But for Somerled, Scotland might have become an extension of Norway, or at least have been controlled by Viking Scandinavians, whether as part of Norway itself, or as an independent Norse country in the west. It was he who brought about the Gaelic revival that eventually crushed the effects of the Norse occupation of the western Highlands and islands.

The state of the population of Scotland about the year 1100 was, roughly, as follows: The northern mainland, Caithness and Sutherland, was Norse, under the control of the Norwegian king. The Norse Kingdom of Man and the Isles, subject to the Kings of Norway and the Kings of Scotland, contained a mixed population, now mainly Norse, although originally Celtic, especially in Man itself. The Hebrides contained the native Scoto-Irish Gaels, now threatened with extinction by the intruding Norsemen. Inevitably the two opposing races gradually intermingled, including the nearly submerged Picts and, by Somerled's time a mixed people, the Gall-Gàidheil, had evolved. They were looked down upon by the purebred Gaels, who held their bloodlines in the highest regard.

The great Celtic province of Moray was home to a wholly Gaelic population, and comprised the area of the modern counties of Ross,

ANCIENT NORTH AND SOUTH ARGYLL

Ancient North Argyll
Area of contention with Norse

Ancient South Argyll
Approximate area of Argyll
in Somerled's day, including
the Argyll Islands

SHETLAND
ISLANDS

ORKNEY
ISLANDS

CAITHNESS

SUTHERLAND

OUTER HEBRIDES

OR WESTERN ISLES OR SUDREYS

SKYE

ROSS

DRUIM ALBAN

Loch Ness

NAIRN

MORAY

SCOTLAND

GIGHA

KINTYRE

ARRAN

IRELAND

NORTHUMBRIA

ISLE OF
MAN

Moray, Nairn and north-east Inverness.

The 'Scotland' of the twelfth century was limited to the area enclosed by the Moray border to the north, the mountains of Druim Alban to the west and Northumbria to the south – a constantly moving border as battles raged to and fro.

It was the tension between Celt and Norseman over possession of the western mainland and islands that exploded into open confrontation between the latter and Somerled, the son of a dispossessed Celtic chief of Argyll, and which led to the eventual expulsion of the Norse from the entire country, now known as Scotland, in the fifteenth century.

So who, exactly, were the enemy?

Is acher ingaith innocht: fufuasna fairge findfolt
Ni agor reimm mora minn dondlaechraid lainn na lothlind

(Bitter is the wind tonight: it tosses the sea's white hair
I do not fear the coursing of a clear sea by the fierce warriors
from Norway)

These lines, written by an unknown Irish monk of the ninth century, give an indication of who the aggressors were. The word 'lothlind' is old Gaelic for 'Lochlann', ie 'Norway', so there was no doubt in his mind as to where the attackers came from.

The word 'Dane' is sometimes used to refer to Norse attackers, both Danish and Norwegian, in the western seaboard but usually 'Dane' refers to the Dubh-Gall (Black Foreigners or Strangers) coming from Denmark to plunder the east coasts of England. Generally speaking most writers agree that the Viking invaders of the northern mainland of Scotland, especially Caithness and Sutherland, and the Western Isles, were Fionn-Gall (White Foreigners or Strangers) or Norwegians.

A wild and stormy sea was indeed often the only protection the Gaels had against the barbaric cruelty of the Vikings, as the Scottish kings appeared impotent or indifferent regarding the west. *Heimskringla*, Magnus Bareleg's Saga, 1098, describes a meeting between King Magnus of Norway and King Malcolm of Scotland in which the kings made peace between them, to the effect that King Magnus should possess all the islands that lie to the west of Scotland between which and the mainland he could go in a ship with the rudder in place.

Magnus very cunningly sat at the helm of a light ship with its rudder in place, and had it drawn across the isthmus between West Loch Tarbert and East Loch Tarbert, thus claiming possession of the considerable peninsula of Kintyre. In fact, at the time of Magnus' expedition Edgar was king of Scotland. Malcolm III had died in 1093. The treaty might have been made with a pretender to the throne. But the intention clearly was that the Norse should stay on the islands and leave the mainland alone, as not only was the king of Scotland too involved with plundering the rich Northumbrian lands to the south, and fending off incursions by challenging Celtic chiefs to the north, but also he obviously considered the west less important and productive than the eastern coasts.

Somerled is reported to have said that when his forefathers were dispossessed by the invasion of the Norsemen they had no assistance to defend or recover their lands, from the Scottish king. We tend to regard terrorism as a modern phenomenon, but the centuries of the Viking invasions were a time of unremitting violence and devastating fear throughout the northern and western seaboards of Scotland, as well as the coasts and islands bordering the Irish Sea. Tales of Viking-inflicted horrors still abound in Scotland, and among the catalogue of commonly known crimes, such as the castration and blinding of men, and the callous massacre of children, there are the shuddering tales of the Blood Eagle, whereby a victim's heart and lungs were torn out from the living body and spread, dripping bloodily, in the form of an eagle wherever they would strike the most terror into the souls of whoever saw them. Such an appalling event is graphically described in *Harald Fairhair's Saga* when Halfdan Longleg was so tortured by his own brother, Einar. Vikings prided themselves on showing no pity as this was regarded as weakness, so it is a sickening irony that the Viking thug, who actually disliked the practice of throwing babies into the air and impaling them on spear points, was known as the 'Bairns Man'.

By the early years of the twelfth century the spirit of the Celtic people of the west was crushed and demoralised under these dreadful conditions. A leader of iron will and determination was needed to encourage them to rise against their oppressors – and that man was Somerled, son of Gillebride, grandson of Gilleadamnan, a young, strong and charismatic chief whose spirit was overwhelmed with rage rather than depression at the situation in which his people found themselves. He had taken part in various abortive attempts by his father, Gillebride, to regain the family's tribal lands in the Morvern district of Argyll, which had been seized by the Norse, probably in King Harald Fairhair's time. Gillebride proved to be a completely ineffectual leader, without his son's latent talent for organisation and strategy which was soon to be demonstrated when Somerled virtually took over the leadership of the remnants of his father's tattered force, allowing Gillebride to retire into depressed obscurity.

But there was more to regaining Morvern than just defeating the Vikings. Many factors were to be considered, and influences to be examined. Argyll, the centre of Somerled's world, was encircled by other powers and kingdoms, all of which would affect his thoughts and actions in the years to come as he increased his status from chief, to King of Argyll and Lord of the Isles.

These influences can perhaps be most clearly seen in the following diagram:

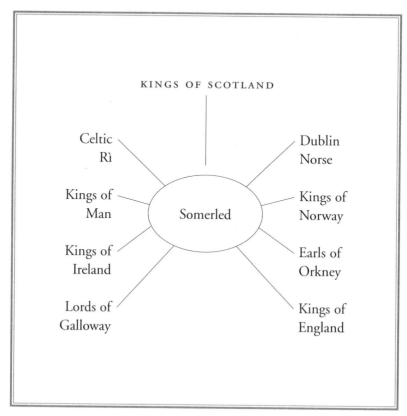

KINGS OF SCOTLAND

Celtic
Rì

Dublin
Norse

Kings of
Man

Somerled

Kings of
Norway

Kings of
Ireland

Earls of
Orkney

Lords of
Galloway

Kings of
England

CHAPTER TWO

Kings of Scotland

The king of Scotland whom Somerled was to have most dealings with throughout his career was David I, son of Malcolm III (Canmore), and his Hungarian-born wife (Saint) Margaret of the royal Wessex line of Alfred. David, having succeeded in 1124, on the death of his brother Alexander I, was well established on the throne of Scotland when Somerled began to make his presence felt in Argyll.

This king, like his brothers Edgar and Alexander before him, was actively pursuing a policy of friendship towards England, particularly so after the marriage of their sister Matilda to the English King Henry I. According to the *Chronicle of Melrose* Donald Ban, Malcolm III's brother, had claimed the kingdom and sent away into exile in England his young nephews, Edgar, Alexander and David. The young heirs were said to have shed their Scottish barbarity and acquired English 'polish', along with English friends, during their sojourn in the south.

The dependence of these three Scottish kings on English support had made them well disposed towards England, and David, on returning to Scotland as king, after a long exile in Romsey Abbey, had brought with him large numbers of his Norman, Flemish and Breton friends, giving them high positions in Church and State, including large estates. Many of those newcomers were to become 'more Scottish than the Scots', eg Bruce, Chisholm, Cumming, Haig, Fraser, Sinclair, Stewart ('from steward'), Soulis, Morville, Melville, Gordon, Gifford, Oliphant, Crichton, Lindsay, Boswell, Montgomery, Maxwell, Balliol, Seton and Somerville.

The peaceful state of relations between England and Scotland meant that David could indulge his desire – probably as a result of his saintly mother's inspiration – to set up many religious institutions and parishes with the purpose of civilising and taming the wild south-eastern and Border lands. Churches and abbeys were founded at

Jedburgh, Dunfermline, Kelso, Newbattle, Kinloss, Melrose, Holyrood and Paisley. This took up much of the king's energy and kept his attention away from the west, as did the 'Normanising' of Scotland – the familiarising of the Scots with the feudal system of landholding and government. Scotland now had contacts with the latest currents of intellectual and religious life pervading western Christendom in the twelfth century.

Also diverting King David's attention from the west was the first serious challenge to his sovereignty from the old Celtic line, descended from Malcolm I and the family of Moray.

Moray was what remained of the old northern Pictish kingdom which had united with the Scots under King Kenneth MacAlpin (840 or 843–58). Since then the throne had passed from king to king by the Law of Tanistry, the Celtic system of succession. The Tanist Law ensured the succession to the throne of the candidate who was considered the most suitable, regardless of whether he was the eldest or not, as long as he was in the senior line of descent, ie his father, grandfather or great-grandfather had been a king. This often resulted in the succession going down not directly, but alternately, between one senior branch of the family and another. In fact, brothers were considered preferable to sons as they were one generation nearer to the founder of the line than were sons.

Tanistry, therefore, provided lateral lines of succession. Primogeniture was introduced in the reigns of the Margaretsons (sons of Malcolm III by Queen Margaret) for the first time.

King Malcolm had broken the Law of Tanistry by killing MacBeth and Lulach of the alternative line, thus, as he thought, ensuring the security of succession of his own sons by his wife Margaret, but the Moray line still existed in the persons of King Lulach's grandsons, Angus and Malcolm (Earls of Moray and Ross, respectively).

The Moray challenge was regarded as both understandable and legitimate by the Highlanders as they considered Queen Margaret's sons to be foreigners. Her 'Englishness' was thought to be remote, though she was of the ancient royal Wessex line of Alfred the Great, as she was born of a Hungarian mother and had been brought up in Hungary. Her son, David I, son of this 'foreign' mother, and brought up in the court of the English King Henry I, seemed more English than Scots, and the influx of Bretons, Normans and Flemings since his father's day infuriated the native Highlanders.

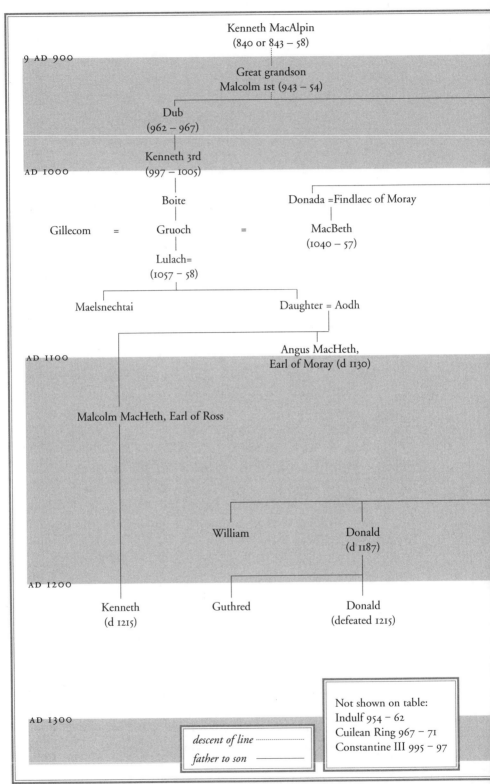

Kenneth MacAlpin
(840 or 843 – 58)

9 AD 900

Great grandson
Malcolm 1st (943 – 54)

Dub
(962 – 967)

Kenneth 3rd
AD 1000   (997 – 1005)

Boite   Donada =Findlaec of Moray

Gillecom   =   Gruoch   =   MacBeth
                                          (1040 – 57)

Lulach=
(1057 – 58)

Maelsnechtai   Daughter = Aodh

Angus MacHeth,
AD 1100   Earl of Moray (d 1130)

Malcolm MacHeth, Earl of Ross

William   Donald
                      (d 1187)

AD 1200

Kenneth   Guthred   Donald
(d 1215)   (defeated 1215)

AD 1300

Not shown on table:
Indulf 954 – 62
Cuilean Ring 967 – 71
Constantine III 995 – 97

descent of line ·········

father to son ─────

Genealogical table of descendants of Kenneth MacAlpin (840 or 843 – 58).

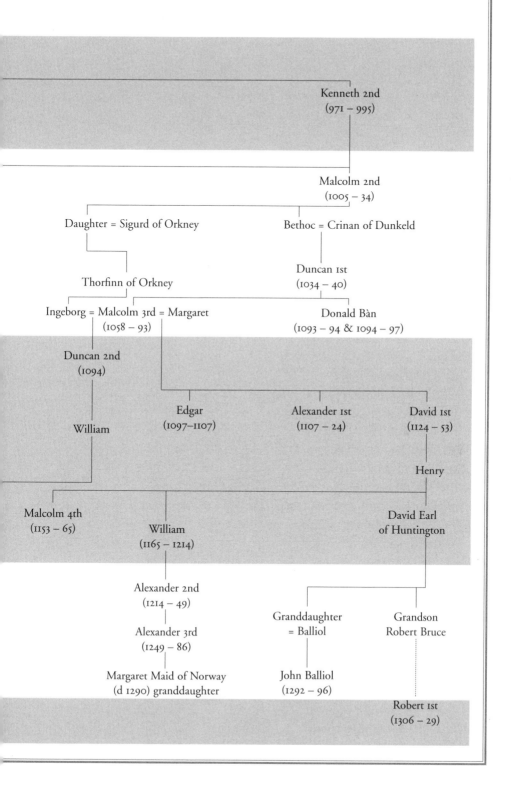

Kenneth 2nd
(971 – 995)

Malcolm 2nd
(1005 – 34)

Daughter = Sigurd of Orkney

Bethoc = Crinan of Dunkeld

Duncan 1st
(1034 – 40)

Thorfinn of Orkney

Ingeborg = Malcolm 3rd = Margaret
(1058 – 93)

Donald Bàn
(1093 – 94 & 1094 – 97)

Duncan 2nd
(1094)

Edgar
(1097–1107)

Alexander 1st
(1107 – 24)

David 1st
(1124 – 53)

William

Henry

Malcolm 4th
(1153 – 65)

William
(1165 – 1214)

David Earl
of Huntington

Alexander 2nd
(1214 – 49)

Alexander 3rd
(1249 – 86)

Granddaughter
= Balliol

Grandson
Robert Bruce

Margaret Maid of Norway
(d 1290) granddaughter

John Balliol
(1292 – 96)

Robert 1st
(1306 – 29)

On the other hand, King Lulach's son, Malsnechtai, was of the senior line of descent from Malcolm I until his death in 1085. He had no heirs male, so the descent continued through the son of his sister and her husband, Aodh, the first Earl of Moray, who was highly regarded at the Scottish Court. Aodh's sons and grandsons were therefore the last representatives of the senior line, and obviously eligible as credible contestants for the Scottish throne under the Tanist System. In Gaelic 'son of Aodh' is rendered 'Mhic Aoidh', and anglicised as MacKay or MacHeth. Angus, Earl of Moray, used the style MacHeth.

The son of Aodh, Angus, was a thorn in the flesh of, firstly King Alexander I, and then of King David I in the year of his accession, 1124. He led rebellions against King David, along with his brother, Malcolm MacHeth, Earl of Ross, but they were unsuccessful. However, Angus and Malcolm again attempted to unseat the king in 1130, during the latter's absence in England. The *Annals of Ulster* report that a battle was fought between the king of Scots' forces and the Moray men, which the Scots won. Four thousand of the Moray men were killed, against one thousand of the Scots, and their leader, Angus, grandson of King Lulach, was among the slain.

Malcolm, in his turn, claimed the throne as a descendant of Lulach. He, however, was captured and imprisoned in Roxburgh Castle. There is much speculation about him; it is said that he was an illegitimate son of Alexander I. The *Chronicle of Stephen* comments that we really have no idea as to Malcolm's parentage, although he is called MacBeth in the *Chronicle of Holyrood.* Orderic Vitalis, a contemporary writer, says he was the illegitimate son of Alexander I, but the Moray claimants always said they were descended from MacBeth. The name 'MacBeth', however, may simply stand for ' religious man', and have no patronymic significance whatever. At any rate, he was imprisoned in Roxburgh from 1134 until his release in 1157, after which he married Somerled's sister. In spite of his rebellious lifestyle he seemed to have been born under a lucky star, for he ended his life as earl of Ross, in 1168.

There is also speculation that he may have been the son of Prince Ethelred, a son of Malcolm Canmore, who was debarred from the throne by being a churchman, but whose own son would not be thus debarred. The confusion is compounded by the mention in the Chronicles of a mysterious and formidable churchman, named

Wimund, who is said to have claimed to be the rightful heir to Moray as an illegitimate son of Alexander I. The *Annals of Innisfallen* refer to the *Chronicles of York* saying that a bishop of the islands, called Wimund, was consecrated by Thomas II, archbishop of York. Wimund declared falsely that he was a son of the earl of Moray ie of Angus, King Lulach's grandson. The chronicles continue that Wimund invaded Scotland after 1130 and say that no positive conclusions can be drawn and that Wimund has also been rashly identified with Malcolm MacHeth or MacBeth.

Whether Malcolm and Wimund were the same person has been, and is, a subject of debate among historians. At any rate Malcolm MacHeth married the sister of Somerled so it would appear that Somerled tacitly agreed with these Highland uprisings, thus involving the Islesmen. But around 1130, when Somerled first comes actively to our notice, the scene of these activities was central Scotland, not the west.

The geography of western Scotland was also an important factor in keeping the kings of Scots out of the area. The western mainland of Scotland was an isolated fortress virtually impenetrable from any landward attack until General Wade started to open it up with his modern road-building programme. This was begun in 1726, as a result of the Jacobite Rebellion of 1715. Difficult terrain and high mountain passes could render futile any attempted infiltration by large armies. The trackless wastes of mountain and moor were ideal only for guerrilla warfare, not for pitched battles, as even the Romans found to their cost. This mountain mass is Druim Alban, the ridge or backbone of Alba (the Gaelic word for Scotland), and was described by Adamnan as the 'hills of the ridge of Britain'. It formed the ancient boundary between the lands of the Picts and those of the Dalriadic Scots. Successive kings of Scots were wary of committing troops to potentially lethal ambush in this highland area.

The coastline of the west is similarly hostile. The western mainland from Galloway to Cape Wrath is cut up into thousands of sea lochs, creeks and bays, affording shelter to those who know their way around, but bringing danger from tide-race, current, overfall, whirlpool, reef and skerry – as well as from hostile defenders – to those who do not. Somerled's own county of Argyll alone has a thousand-mile, heavily indented coastline, and this without including the islands. In Somerled's day the king of Scots had no fleet to match that of the ubiquitous Norsemen, nor that of Somerled himself at the height of his power around 1160.

There seems to have been no organised resistance to the Norse from the Scottish kings following King Kenneth MacAlpin (who united the Picts and the Dalriadic Scots in 847 or 848), for these kings were involved in almost perpetual warfare, not only with their territorial neighbours in the east and south-east of Scotland, but also with invading Danes attacking the richer east coasts of Britain. As the north and west coasts of Scotland were less productive, but very similar to the coasts of Norway, the Norsemen tended to confine themselves to these areas, which were of less concern to the Scottish kings than their principal territories in the east. So the west and north tended to be left alone to defend themselves as best they could, or come to terms with the raiding, and eventually colonising, Norsemen.

CHAPTER THREE

The Norse Kingdom
of Man and the Isles

Apart from the Norse and the king of Scots, another factor in the politics of the west was undoubtedly Olaf, King of Man and the Isles, whose friendship was to be of vital significance to Somerled.

According to the *Chronicle of Man*, the ruler of the kingdom was variously known as Olaf the Red, Olaf Morsel or Olaf Bitling. There is doubt about the exact years of his reign, which are given as 1103–53, or 1104–54, in the sometimes unreliable *Chronicle of Man*. It says that Olaf, the son of Godred or Godfrey Crovan of Man, ruled for forty years, but the same *Chronicle* places Olaf's death under 1143–53, so the word 'forty' seems here an error for 'fifty'.

The extent of his kingdom, by Somerled's time, was the archipelago of islands from Man to Lewis, with a population of Norse, Gall-Gàidheil and indigenous Celt – an uneasy mix in a geographically complex area. Olaf had inherited this well-established kingdom, under the suzerainty of Norway and Scotland, from his typically Norse, land-grabbing father, Godred Crovan, but Olaf himself comes over as a shrewd and rather mild-mannered, peace-loving man in an era when violence prevailed in the western islands. Indeed the *Chronicle of Man* described him as a peaceable man who had made careful alliances with the Irish and Scottish kings in order to avoid any threat to his island kingdom. It was from the kingdom of Man and the Isles that the later Lordship of the Isles was to originate.

RL Bremner's *The Norsemen in Alban* gives the opinion that the Lordship of the Isles was held first by the Danes of Limerick, from the time of Ketil Flatnose, around 890 AD. He adds that the first kings of the Gall-Gàidheil, or kings of Man and the Isles, were direct descendants of Ivar Beinlaus, the son of Lagmar Lodbrok, and that their chief seat was the Isle of Man. From the beginning the kingdom of the Gall-Gàidheil was tributary to the kings of Norway, and ten gold marks were paid to each king on his accession. Later, these lesser kings were called kings of Man and the Isles. This was Olaf's title when he first met Somerled.

Olaf came to his kingdom as follows: In the year 880 King Harald Haarfagr (Fairhair) of Norway established himself as the first king of Norway but behaved so violently that many of his rivals and their followers sailed 'west over sea' and escaped to the Isles, from where they subsequently carried out pirate attacks on their former homeland. King Harald came after them in force and, having crushed the opposition, added the Isles to the crown of Norway. He sent Ketil Flatnose, a Norwegian aristocrat, to hold the Isles in subjection to him, but this backfired when Ketil declared himself king of the Isles in 890. However, by about 900 all trace of Ketil had disappeared. The next king of the Isles seems to have been Godred MacSitric (or Sigtryggsson), followed by his son, Fingal.

After the Battle of Stamford Bridge in 1066, Harald Hardradi, king of Norway, and his ally, Godred Crovan (the White-handed), son of Harald the Black of Iceland, were defeated in their attempt against William of Normandy. The *Chronicle of Man* tells how Godred Crovan fled, after the battle, to seek sanctuary and aid from Godfrey MacSitric, ruler of Man. The Chronicle continues that in 1070 the latter died, and was succeeded by his son, Fingal, and that in 1075 the acquisitive and treacherous Godred Crovan led two unsuccessful expeditions against Fingal of Man, then a third successful one, after which he expelled Fingal and became ruler of the whole of Man. This king was the progenitor of the dynasty of Man and the Isles. He reigned over Man for about 16 years, and also subjugated Dublin and part of Leinster, then fought against King Malcolm III of Scotland. He had three sons, Lagman, Harald and Olaf (Olaf Bitling).

King Magnus Bareleg of Norway made three expeditions to the Isles, in 1093, 1098 and 1103, attacking the Orkneys, Lewis, Skye, the Uists, Mull, Tiree, Islay, Man and Anglesey, and subjugating them. He expelled Crovan and put his son, Sigurd, into the Isles as king. Crovan appears to have been driven out of Dublin about 1094, and to have died in Islay about 1095, as reported in the *Annals of Innisfallen*. Meanwhile, the *Chronicle of Man* informs us that Lagman, son of Crovan, was king in the Hebrides with Sigurd's consent, for seven years, and Sigurd returned to Norway. When Lagman died there was a power vacuum in the Isles, and the islanders applied to Muirchertach, High King of Ireland, to name a suitable prince of his blood (O'Brien) to take control until Olaf

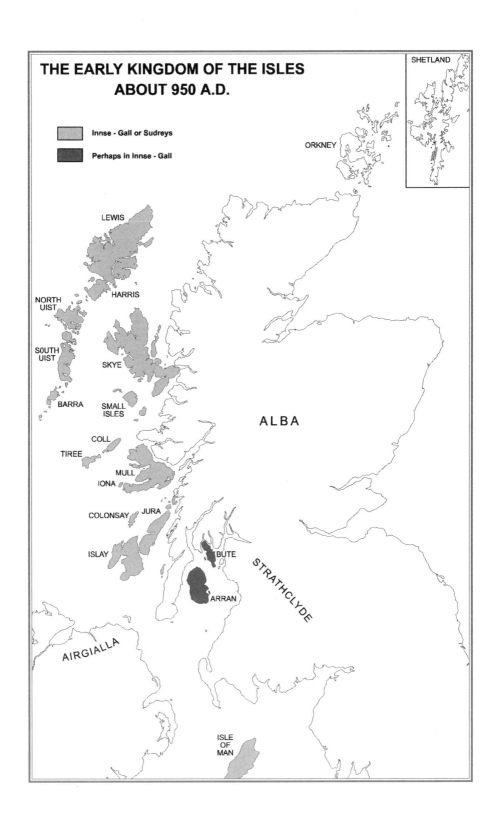

THE EARLY KINGDOM OF THE ISLES
ABOUT 950 A.D.

Innse - Gall or Sudreys

Perhaps in Innse - Gall

SHETLAND

ORKNEY

LEWIS

NORTH UIST

HARRIS

SOUTH UIST

SKYE

BARRA

SMALL ISLES

ALBA

COLL

TIREE

MULL

IONA

COLONSAY   JURA

ISLAY

BUTE

STRATHCLYDE

ARRAN

AIRGIALLA

ISLE OF MAN

was old enough to reign. Donald MacTadc was chosen, but reigned so tyrannically for three years that the island chiefs finally drove him out. At last, Olaf became king of Man and the Isles, and reigned for 50 years.

The term Rìgh Fhionngall (King of the White Strangers) referred originally to the lords of the Norwegian invaders and was frequently applied to the Lords of the Isles. It seems to prove that Olaf, from whom they descended by way of Ragnhildis, his daughter, and Somerled's wife, was styled as such, and it would also seem that his subjects in the Isles, when not Celtic, were Norwegian.

He deliberately cultivated friendship with anyone who might harm his kingdom, and so paid homage to the king of Norway on his accession, leaving his son, Godred (the Black), as a hostage, to be educated in Norway.

Somerled was to become an ally and friend of Olaf through his marriage to Ragnhildis, Olaf's daughter, in 1140, and no doubt benefited from a benign co-existence with the Manx kingdom. It is possible that he would not have attained his later position of supreme power in islands without the tacit support and approval of Olaf. On the other hand Somerled was to become useful to Olaf in that his great seapower would discourage any potential rival Norse aggression towards Man, without Olaf himself having to become actively, and expensively, involved. So the situation was mutually advantageous.

The Norse were undoubtedly masters of all things relating to the sea and ships, and Olaf was a typical Norseman in this respect. He possessed a large fleet of ocean-going ships, with thoroughly efficient shipmasters, which controlled the seas in which his kingdom lay. The Norse had finely designed, clinker-built ships when the much more highly civilised Celts of Ireland and Scotland were paddling around in vulnerable curraghs. Norse settlements in Celtic areas can easily be traced from the maritime vocabulary of coastal place names first seen by Viking raiders arriving

	Norse	to	Gaelic
Lewis	4		1
Islay	1		2
Kintyre	1		7
Man	1		7.5
Arran	1		8

from the sea, eg Brodick – Breidr vik (Broad harbour); Uig – Vik (Sea harbour); Aros – Aross (River mouth); Stemnish – Straumnes (Current-ness).

Also the varied extent of Norse colonisation in the islands can be seen by the ratio of Norse to Gaelic names. Names are discussed in greater detail in chapter 20.

From these ratios it is obvious that the Inner Hebrides were much less 'Norsised' than the Outer Hebrides, which were significantly known as the Innse-Gall (Isles of the Foreigners or Strangers ie Norsemen).

CHAPTER FOUR

No Threat From England – Yet!

The three English kings whose reigns ran concurrently with the main events of Somerled's life were Henry I (Beauclerc), 1100–35; Stephen, 1135–54 and Henry II, 1154–89.

King David's sister, Matilda, had married Henry I, with whom he was on good terms, and as Somerled and David were also on good terms there seemed to be no immediate threat to either Somerled or Olaf from these two kings.

In the early years of the twelfth century new ideas associated with the Gregorian reform movement now threatened traditional rights over the Church and Henry became preoccupied with trying to maintain the lay investiture of new abbots and bishops in the face of Papal prohibition of such practice. Henry couldn't afford to antagonise the great men of the Church, who were also considerable landowners and key administrators. He would always need their assistance in administering his kingdom and wanted to be sure of their continued loyalty. This was no time, therefore, for him to become distracted with events in mainland Scotland, far less in the remote Highlands and islands.

Also, by maintaining a friendly attitude towards the north Henry was making sure that he would not be attacked from that direction while he had his hands full in the south. In addition to Church matters he was occupied with affairs in Normandy and the political instability caused by his brother Robert's attempts to seize the throne, using Normandy as a power base from which to mount attacks on England.

This friendly attitude was the means of saving the Scottish king's throne in 1130 when David was out of the country visiting the English court. Orderic Vitalis, the English chronicler tells us that while David was away, Scotland was attacked by five thousand Moray men, under the command of Angus, Earl of Moray and his brother, Malcolm, in an attempt to gain the Scottish throne. The situation was saved by a counter-attack by David's English cousin, Edward, who routed the enemy, killed Angus, pursued the rebels back into Moray and imposed the king's law on that district.

Thanks to English intervention David's authority was restored, and it ensured the gratitude of David whenever Henry might need his intervention and moral support. Events in the west could take their course while the kings of Scotland and of England were otherwise engaged.

Henry was now mainly concerned with holding on to the power and land he already held, notably Normandy. After 1106 he spent more than half the remainder of his reign dealing with trouble from France, Anjou and Flanders, and finally the rest of his reign trying to ensure the succession of his daughter Matilda – his only living, legitimate child – after the death of his son, William in the sinking of the White Ship in 1120. When Matilda's husband, the Emperor Henry V of Germany, died in 1125, she was recalled to his court by her father. The *Chronicle of Symeon of Durham* describes how, after Christmas 1126, King Henry demanded that his most senior nobles and churchmen, as well as King David of Scotland, should promise to support the claim of his daughter, Matilda, as the legal heir to the throne, unless, of course, a son should be born to him before he died.

As Matilda was David's niece (the daughter of his sister, Matilda, Queen of England), David's support for Henry was further guaranteed. From now on the Scottish king's attention was to be focused, almost constantly, on affairs in England and central Scotland. The Norse presence in the west was almost irrelevant to him and Somerled could, almost certainly, not look for practical assistance from that quarter.

This was the situation in 1130 when Somerled made his bid for power in far-away Argyll. Neither indirectly, through interference in Scottish affairs, nor directly in Isles affairs, did Henry I pose any threat to the remote kingdom of Man and the Isles, though some of his Norman barons may have had different ideas.

CHAPTER FIVE

Viking Terrorists

In 1130 King Sigurd of Norway, son of the renowned King Magnus Bareleg, died. As well as lord of Norway itself he had been suzerain of divers islands and territories which, because of their scattered geography, made them difficult to control and administer, especially as the Norsemen were noted for disobedience towards their kings and for falling out among themselves. This was a disunited realm, and King Sigurd needed to gather in the reins of his scattered empire. Sigurd had also been, in name at any rate, king over Iceland, the settlements in Greenland, the Nordreys (Orkney and Shetland), the mainland territories of Caithness and Sutherland, the lesser kingdom of Man and the Isles including the Sudreys or Western Isles or Outer Hebrides or Innse-Gall, and the province of Ulster.

He had, however, fragmented the kingdom of Norway by giving parts of it to his brothers Eystein and Olaf, who died before him. After his enthusiastic empire-building, Sigurd was followed by his son, Magnus IV, 1130–35, who became joint ruler with Harald IV Gille, 1130–36 (who claimed to be the bastard son of Magnus III). Harald ousted Magnus but was then killed, and the kingdom divided up among petty princes (Sigurd II Munn, 1136–55; Inge I Krokrygg, 1136–61 and Eystein III Haraldsson, 1142–57). These unsettled affairs kept the kings involved at home in Norway and prevented any large scale aggression by a royal Norwegian fleet against Man and the Isles, as no doubt did the presence of Godred the Black, King Olaf Bitling's son, as hostage at the Norwegian court.

In fact, by 1130 the damage to Somerled's patrimony at the hands of the Norwegian kings had been well and truly done, starting as far back as 858 and the death of King Kenneth MacAlpin, first king of the Picts and the Dalriadic Scots. After this there was no organised Scottish resistance to the Norse until Somerled's arrival. Events in Norway then combined to produce a climate ready for early Norse expansion.

The Norse had come originally on plundering expeditions in the long daylight hours and calm, smooth seas of summertime. The easy access to islands and mainland coasts by way of inlets, bays, sea lochs and river mouths made the north and west of Scotland soft targets for the expertly handled longships which could be rowed into tight spaces where manoeuvring under sail was not possible. These versatile vessels did not necessarily require deep water for their keels, but could be beached on shallow, sandy shores and refloated on the next tide.

Scandinavia was rich in iron ore which provided high quality weapons, and iron timber-bolts and keels for ships. The invention of effective tools, such as the axe and the adze made possible the felling of trees and the honing and shaping of tree trunks into lengths suitable for building the sleek, finely designed longships with their extra buoyancy from overlapping planking.

RL Bremner, author of *The Norsemen in Alban*, 1923, whose admiration for all things Norse is rather excessive, says that it seems clear that the Vikings were exploring the western seas before the end of the eighth century. His attitude to the unprovoked attacks on the unsuspecting Scottish coasts is incredibly biased towards the Vikings, whom, unbelievably, he describes in the most fulsome terms, almost as if they were little more than a band of rugby players out for a good time.

Most people, however, utterly condemn a supposedly Christian society which could condone, and even encourage, the barbaric thuggery of its young men, in the lands 'west beyond the sea'. Their claims to fame were the torture, slaughter and rape of innocents, the widespread devastation of homes, animals and lands, the destruction or theft of irreplaceable documents and artefacts from monasteries and churches, and the commonly practised evil of carrying off members of communities to be sold as slaves.

The damage inflicted on the Pictish and Gaelic communities in the west is incalculable, as irreplaceable manuscripts and other cultural artefacts were destroyed or otherwise lost to us for ever. At this point the Picts were virtually submerged under a flood of Scandinavian ingression, while the very existence of the Gael was threatened with extinction. This last, fortunately, was to be reversed as a result of Somerled's activities.

Eighth-century Norway had a problem of lebensraum, like Hitler's Nazi Germany centuries later. The population was growing, the productive land was overcrowded and overstretched as regards the growing of crops, and there was little trade with other countries, especially before the invention of the longship. Farming gradually became unviable because of the wasteful system of land inheritance. Good farming units became fragmented by being divided up on the death of each landowner. This is comparable to the Celtic system of Gavelkind, whereby, on the death of a chief or head of a house, the land was divided among those of consanguinity who were entitled to a share.

Inevitably food became scarcer, with more and more people trying to live on smaller and smaller units of land. The subsequent poverty and shortage of food led to the first exodus of land-hungry Norwegians out of Hordaland into the easily reached islands of Orkney and Shetland. There, any native Celtic population had either to make way for the incomers, or leave. Having colonised these islands successfully, the Norse began to look around for other islands to occupy, and the Hebrides, with a record of more than two hundred years of almost unbroken peace, were plums ripe for the picking.

No doubt land settlement was the motive for many of the first invaders, but the much less honourable one of stealing moveable estate – other people's moveable estate – steadily became an additional attraction, as well as seizing prisoners to be sold as slaves or held for ransom. Piracy was regarded as a summer ploy, with considerable potential for personal enrichment. Ketil Flatnose, King Harald Fairhair's lieutenant, in the *Saga of the Laxdalers*, said that he preferred to sail 'west beyond the sea' to Scotland, as he had sailed there often and knew there were rich pickings for the taking.

The Norse movement westward seemed part of the general long-term movement of Teutonic tribes from the fourth century onwards and led to opportunities for trade to open up, very much so among the Scandinavians, by the late eighth and early ninth centuries. Conditions were now right for change. The Norwegians had iron. They also had vast oak and spruce forests. They had the motive and the stimulus – the need for land, for trade, for expansion, for colonies and empire. And they now had the means to achieve their aims – ships, especially longships. Now they could venture into the hitherto unknown Atlantic, across to the northern and western isles of Scotland and down the westward Scottish coasts, rather than south down the east coasts of Scotland and England. It must have been irresistible. It was an easy voyage from the Norwegian coast to Scotland, achievable within a day's sail and scarcely out of sight of land the whole way. They could easily find the way, as so many had already sailed these waters before them and could pass on the information.

And so the reign of terror began.

The *Annals of Ulster* record the first Viking raid in 793 on Lindisfarne; then in 794 they tell us of the devastation of the whole of Britain by the Vikings, including burning and pillaging throughout the islands of Rathlin and Skye. The *Annals of Innisfallen* report that in 795 Iona suffered its first horrific attack, and that from 796–98 it was the turn of Ireland, including Ulster and the Hebrides. The year 798 saw Man attacked and widespread plundering in Ireland and Scotland, and in 802 Iona was burned again, the Vikings knowing that all that had been stolen and destroyed on the previous raid would have been replaced and restored. The wholesale destruction of monasteries and manuscripts by the Vikings retarded the progress of civilisation – the massacre of Iona was probably the worst misfortune to befall the world of letters as it is impossible to exaggerate the importance of Celtic learning to the western world, Celtic missionaries having left their mark everywhere in Europe.

The *Annals of Ulster* record yet another attack on Iona in 806. On this occasion the raiders killed all 68 monks. By this time the Community had had enough as the island, having been completely devastated yet again, now lay in ruins. The *Annals* tell us of the building of the new monastery of Columcille in Kells, County Meath, and that Cellach, Abbot of Iona, decided in 807 to move to Ireland with what remained of his people.

King Kenneth MacAlpin moved his centre of government to the relative safety of Scone in the central Highlands and established new religious headquarters at Dunkeld. From here Kenneth set out to consolidate his power in as much of old Pictland as he could hold against the Norsemen, and thus created the kingdom of the Picts and the Scots which was to survive the Viking Age. But from their island bases the Vikings attacked Kenneth's kingdom and fought over littoral bases whose names eg Ullapool and Eriboll, show their Norse origin.

There is a heavy density of Norse names around the Kyle of Tongue and, of course, across the plain of Caithness which was closer to the power base of Orkney. The Norse eventually held not only Caithness but also Southland, now known as Sutherland, which was originally the coastal plain along the Moray Firth below the cliffs of

Caithness. They established their centre at Dingwall from where they could conveniently attack Pictish and Scottish settlements in the north-east. However, they seemed to have been impartial as to where and whom they raided, whether Scots, Irish, Welsh or English – and also many of their own people's settlements on the Scottish mainland and islands.

Swein, a Viking who accompanied King Magnus Bareleg on his expedition to the Hebrides, is extolled by one of the Court skalds thus:

Half-a-dozen homesteads burning
Half-a-dozen homesteads plundered
This was Swein's work of a morning

It seems only fitting that Swein was killed by Danish Vikings while raiding their settlement of Dublin!

The year 825 saw Iona attacked by Vikings looking for treasure, and the martyrdom in the church of Blathmac, son of Fland, a Christian Irish prince and general. Every day was fear-laden in case of the dreaded appearance of the great rectangular sails with their raven device. The brutal atrocities of the Viking Age dragged on, seemingly endlessly throughout the years from 797 until 836 when the intensity of attacks made it the most agonising year of all. But, miraculously, the Church and the people drew together for comfort and courage and, incredibly, Christianity survived in the face of the heathen onslaught.

By this time the Norsemen had annexed the Western Isles, Sutherland and Caithness, but were fractured into mutually hostile factions. Each 'gang' gave service only to its own chief, and each gang was out for itself. The idea of a single unified force under one great leader was not part of the Viking psyche. This was their weakness and led to their ultimate failure to hold on to the widespread Norwegian colonial empire which stretched from the Northern Isles to Ireland.

In addition, the Norsemen were top-notch sailors, and gave service to their chiefs in terms of ships and oar-power, but were not the stuff of conquering armies. By this time Diarmit, Abbot of Iona and later of Kells, had taken the precious relics of Columba to Scotland, and then in 831 to Ireland. After 836 the fashion for going-a-viking seemed to fade somewhat, and things were changing politically in Norway.

Around 872, Harald Haarfagre (Fairhair), the most formidable Norwegian personality of the ninth century, seized supreme power in splintered Norway, after the Battle of Hafrsfiordr, and forcibly fused it into a single monarchy and something resembling a modern state. These high-handed and get-tough methods inevitably displeased many of his subjects who promptly began an exodus to the Nordreys, the newly discovered Iceland and the Western Isles, from which useful bases they carried out retaliatory raids on their former homeland.

It was during Harald's lifetime that the Norse colonisation of Scottish territory definitely began with the settlement of homeless Norsemen in the Orkney Islands. It was Harald's desire to crush the raiders effectively that led to his first expedition to Scotland around the year 874, as described in *Harald Fairhair's Saga*. No resistance was offered. He went first to Shetland and Orkney where he killed every Viking who had not fled before him; then went on to the Hebrides where he plundered and killed any opposition. Everywhere he went he fought, and won.

The *Landnámabók* describes how Harald made another, much more formidable, attack on the islands about 20 years later, and subdued all the Hebrides. He acquired more territories overseas than any other Norse king, except Magnus Bareleg in later days, but when he departed with his fleet from Hebridean waters Scots and Irish pirates plundered the Hebrides after him. When Harald was informed about this he sent Ketil Flatnose, a Norwegian chief, to take over the Western Isles again, in his name.

The *Eyrbyggia Saga* reports that this was done, but that Ketil came to relish his relative independence of action so far distant from the King's immediate reach, and that he sent no taxes back to Harald, declared himself to be king of the Hebrides and, in fact, established an empire which was to survive until 1469, when the last of the Isles were returned to Scotland. As a result Harald seized Ketil's Norwegian lands making the latter decide to leave Norway for good. From about 900 it appears that the Gall-Gàidheil fusion was truly taking place, as is seen in personal names, eg Aulaf MacSitric (son of the Danish king of Northumberland), Marcus MacArailt (his nephew) and Gofra MacArailt (a possible ancestor of Somerled). The use of 'Mac' (Gaelic 'son') is significant in among otherwise Scandinavian names.

During this time the Church on the Scottish west coast and in the islands may have had a unifying effect on its members, but such was not always the case in the Norse communities.

The Church struggled to restrain them, and the kings or Norway to dominate them. On the whole religious authority was the more acceptable, being the lesser of two evils. The colonists attempted as much independence from Norway as the situation allowed. Orkney, for example, became a power base for disaffected Norsemen, and would gradually increase in strategic importance, and eventually evolve into the earldom of Orkney. In the meantime, however, the Norwegian kings demanded tribute, and tended to get it, by fair means or foul.

Even the Gall-Gàidheil chiefs of the Isle of Man, although having achieved the status of kings of Man and the Isles, were still tribute to the kings of Norway, paying ten gold marks to each king on his accession. By the mid-eleventh century the Norse domination in the west and north was at its greatest strength, and the king of Norway had more control over this part of Scotland than had the king of Scotland himself.

By now the archipelago of the western islands had become a recognised kingdom with a real sense of identity, its people describing themselves as Islesmen, not Scots, Norwegians or Irish, and by the time of the arrival in 1093 of Magnus III (Barrfett or Bareleg) on the throne of Norway there was common cause among the Isles, especially under Godred Crovan (see section on Man) to break away from Norway and Scotland, and become an autonomous kingdom and sovereign state. Unfortunately, they had not reckoned with the ambitious mind of the king of Norway, the greatest Norwegian sovereign since Harald Fairhair over two centuries previously. He was to have a profound effect on Somerled's future kingdom. This was a young, vigorous and ambitious king with a fanatical pride in Norse glory, who was determined to make his royal authority felt in the old Norse empire, especially as the king of Scotland was otherwise engaged.

He set out ruthlessly to regain areas where he felt Norse power had been eroded, and made three punitive expeditions 'west over sea' in 1093, 1098 and 1102-3, attacking the Orkneys, Lewis, Skye, the Uists, Mull, Tiree, Islay, Man and Anglesey.

His progress, in 1098, with a large fleet of 160 ships is easily traced. This was not the visit of a kindly patriarch to show his subjects the error of their ways, but that of a harsh despot intent on punishing his perceived enemies, and his voyage was marked by a trail of blood, fire and terror. His methods of gaining respect actually earned him undying hatred and are well recorded in the sagas.

Magnus Bareleg's Saga tells us how Magnus sailed to the Hebrides where he immediately began to plunder and burn the inhabited isles, killing the people wherever he found them. As many as were able fled far and wide, some into Scotland, and some south, via Kintyre, to Ireland. Those remaining, who did homage, had their lives spared.

The Outer Isles and the Argyll islands seem to have suffered most – his Saga says that he left smoke over Islay, and Tiree and Mull experienced the full force of this wrath:

In Lewis Isle with fearful blaze
The house-destroying fire plays;
To hills and rocks the people fly
Fearing all shelter but the sky.
In Uist the king deep crimson made
the lightning of his glancing blade;
The peasant lost his land and life
Who dared to bide the Norseman's strife.

The hungry battle-birds were filled
in Skye with blood of foemen killed,
and wolves on Tiree's lonely shore
Dyed red their hairy jaws in gore.
The men of Mull were tired of flight;
The Scottish foemen would not fight
And many an island girl's wail
Was heard as through the Isles we sail.

On Sanda's plain our shields they spy;
From Islay smoke rose heaven-high,
Whirling up from the flashing blaze
The king's men o'er the island raised
South of Kintyre the people fled
Scared by our swords in blood dyed red,
And our brave champion onward goes
To meet in Man the Norsemen's foes.

BY BJORN CRIPPLEHAND
COURT POET TO KING MAGNUS BARELEG

The exception, however, was Iona, for this island by now had sacred associations for the Norsemen who were, at least nominally, Christians.

When he arrived in Iona Magnus behaved with uncharacteristic mildness towards all the islanders, and he also displayed a reverence, rare in a Norseman, when he would neither enter himself, nor allow anyone else to enter, the church of Columba. He then sailed on to Wales and killed Earl Hugh, causing the Welsh army to flee in disorder, and captured the island of Anglesey, which was the most southerly of all Norwegian conquests.

And where were the king of Scots and his army during Magnus' campaigns of devastation and slaughter? Malcolm III was bent on attacking northern England after failed peace negotiations with King William II, and the impending attack, which was to lead to his death in 1093, was obviously enough to prevent him taking active measures against Magnus. We may accept as authentic the Norse reference to negotiations for a settlement between the two kings, as described in the *Heimskringla*, to the effect that King Magnus should possess all the islands that lie to the west of Scotland, that is, the Sudreys, provided he could go between them and the mainland in a ship with her rudder in place. The intention was clearly that the Norse should stay solely in the Isles, leaving the mainland as a recognised part of the Scottish kingdom. This arrangement, convenient as it was at the time, was going to cause bitter resentment in Somerled and in later Scottish kings against the unwelcome Norse presence on the western seaboard, especially as it had been made with the actual agreement of the Scottish king. Magnus, being an astute man and an opportunist, and wishing to obtain the Kintyre peninsula for its fertile land, the best in the Hebrides (except for Man), decided to fulfil the letter, if not the spirit of the arrangement, by causing his men to pull a ship with her rudder in place, across the isthmus of Kintyre. Magnus sat in the steersman's place holding the steering-oar, and thus claimed possession of the whole of Kintyre.

The death of Malcolm Canmore in 1093, and the disunion in Scotland which followed the disputed succession, prevented any attempt being made to reverse this Norse trickery over Kintyre. Magnus made sure of his newly ceded lands by showing the flag and remaining in the Hebrides all winter. Then he took his ships throughout all the west coast firths and islands, claiming them all in the name of the king of Norway.

The deputies left by Magnus to administer the islands did so so badly that the islanders revolted, leading to Magnus' third expedition to the Isles in 1102-3, then on to Man and further, to Ireland, where he became over-confident and careless, and was killed at the young age of 30.

If Magnus had lived longer, Norse control over the Isles, and Argyll in particular, might have been much greater, as he had been determined to force his scattered empire into a unified whole by endeavouring to conciliate – but with overhanging threats – his new subjects and his former enemies. These events bring us into the era of Somerled, probably an infant at this time. The Sudreys remained tributary to Norway for the next 150 years. Meanwhile the Islesmen sent for Olaf Godredsson, also known as Olaf the Red, or Bitling or Morsel, to be king of Man and the Isles. He controlled this kingdom until the rise of Somerled in 1130 changed the situation for good.

CHAPTER SIX

Celtic Rì

The Rì were the seven great mormaers, or earls, of Scotland (Rì is an abbreviation of 'Rìgh', the Gaelic word for 'King') and they all paid fealty to the Ard Rìgh, the High King of Scots, to whom they were obliged to offer service when required. But it was these lesser Rì who actually appointed the Ard Rìgh, elected from the members of the Royal House, according to the ancient Tanist System.

Their origins are losts in the mists of time but it seems that, although inferior in rank to the High King, they were not created each time by him. Instead, each succeeded by descent to his title, and was confirmed, or otherwise, on coming to pay fealty at the inauguration of every new High King.

The territories of the Rì are uncertain, but W F Skene's *Picts and Scots* suggests the following traditional, ancient divisions of Scotland: Angus and the Mearns; Atholl and Gowrie; Strathearn and Mentieth; Fife; Mar and Buchan; Moray and Ross and, finally, Caithness.

Twelfth-century representation of the seven earldoms tended to leave out Caithness, which was in the hands of the Norse from the beginning of the Dark Ages, and listed the territories as Fife, Strathearn, Angus, Mar, Buchan, Moray and Ross (Ross actually being part of the larger earldom of Moray).

Argyll appears in neither list and Somerled does not seem to have regarded himself as one of the Rì, but as an independent king, or regulus, in the west. This title descended by way of Suibhne MacAnrahan, brother of the High King of Ireland, who built Castle Sween in the late eleventh century. His claim to the title seems to be that he married a princess of the House of Argyll, gaining Cowal and Knapdale as her dowry, and promptly assumed the title regulus, or sub-king, of the Isles. It is not known which king – that of Scotland, Ireland or Norway – was his overlord.

This placed Somerled – as an almost autonomous ruler – in the unique position of being infinitely valuable to both the Rì and the

ANCIENT LAND DIVISIONS OF THE RÌ

SHETLAND

ORKNEY

CAITHNESS

ROSS

MORAY

BUCHAN

MAR

MEARNS

ATHOLL

ANGUS

GOWRIE

STRATHEARN

FIFE

MENTEITH

GALLOWAY

kings of Scots, as a possible ally, and allowed him to play what was to become a dangerous power game with these two factions.

The seven districts covered that area of Scotland regarded as the Celtic North, and were radically different from the 'Scotland' ruled over by the kings of Scots. They constituted almost a separate country, being totally Gaelic-speaking and tribal. Scotland and the North existed uneasily side by side, neither trusting the other and existing mainly in a state of armed neutrality. The Rì regarded themselves almost as equals of the High King whom, after all, they elected, and jealousy guarded their own individual power and style. Until the Middle Ages most kings of Scots were glad to keep out of the North with its impassable mountains and glens where royal armies rarely fought pitched battles and where guerrilla tactics were the most effective form of warfare.

The High King of Scots was frequently disregarded in the North where the Rì were all-powerful kings in their own areas. In fact, the High King was often completely unknown to the majority of clansmen. So it was a point of weakness in the kingdom that the king could never really be sure of the loyalty of the Rì, who remained always an unknown quantity, and if Argyll were ever to unite with the North against the sovereign he was in real danger of being overthrown.

The Rì were very antagonistic towards the growth of Norman power during the reign of David I, and especially during that of Malcolm IV (the Maiden) who absented himself from Scotland in order to placate Henry II of England, to whom he paid homage, thus compromising Scotland's independence.

Likewise the Rì were the focus of the dislike and distrust of the Normans, Bretons and Flemings at court – a potential threat to all that the incomers had acquired since coming to Scotland – and a possible threat to the very source of their power and wealth, the throne of Scotland itself. The newcomers included Somerled in their antagonism to all things Celtic.

As for how the king himself reacted – Somerled against the Vikings was most acceptable, but Somerled in alliance with the Rì presented the possibility of a pincer movement around the very heart of Scotland and danger to the throne. The potential fighting power of the united Celtic North with the Argyll and Hebridean forces was always a nightmare to the sovereigns to Scotland, and it was the assumption of this deadly alliance that brought matters to a head in 1164 when

Somerled brought his renowned fleet up the Firth of Clyde and threatened to overwhelm the central belt of Scotland and the forces of the king of Scotland.

It was, without doubt, the unexplained non-appearance of the unpredictable Celtic Rì, at this critical moment, which was to lead to the ultimate disaster at Bargarran, near Renfrew and the death of Somerled.

CHAPTER SEVEN

Affairs in Ireland

The fifth century had seen the disintegration of the old Roman Empire and the populations of Europe on the move, among them the Gaelic Celts from Irish Dalriada (Antrim) to Scottish Dalriada, the later Argyll. It has been said that no Scot ever landed in Britain except from a ship from Ireland and many a Scottish clan chief claimed descent from the ancient Ulster warrior aristocracy, among them Somerled MacGillebride, progenitor of the great Clan Donald.

There had been much coming and going between Ireland and Scotland perhaps even as early as the fourth century BC, and many place names in Argyll show evidence of early settlements of Gaels from Ireland. These were established as a result of battles fought through the centuries, over the possession of lands in Dalriada, and Argyll as a whole. Irish mythology, as told by the bards of the *beul aithris* (oral tradition), claims the descent of Clan Donald from Conn Cheud Chath, Ard Rìgh Eireann (Conn of the Hundred Battles, High King of Ireland), who ruled from 177-212 AD. There is even an old tale that he fought a battle in Kintyre.

The very name Dalriada refers us to the three Irish Riata brothers, including the princely Cairbre who, because of famine, left their home in Munster and, with family and friends, set out for the Dalriada coast, that is, the northern part of Antrim that lies to the north of the Glenravel River, where they forcibly took the land and settled it. This was the original Irish Dalriada, or 'Riata's portion'. Bede tells us that Cairbre Riata later crossed through the present North Channel into the Firth of Clyde, to Scotland in 258, and settled in lands in Argyll, which also held the name Dalriada, for many centuries. Cairbre Riata is suggested to have been the son of the Irish High King, Conaire Moglama, in the mid-third century, and to have descended from Fergus MacFerdach, supposed progenitor of the kingdom of the Scots. It has also been suggested that he was merely an eponymous hero and not a real person.

Whether this is true or not the name stuck, and there is plenty of

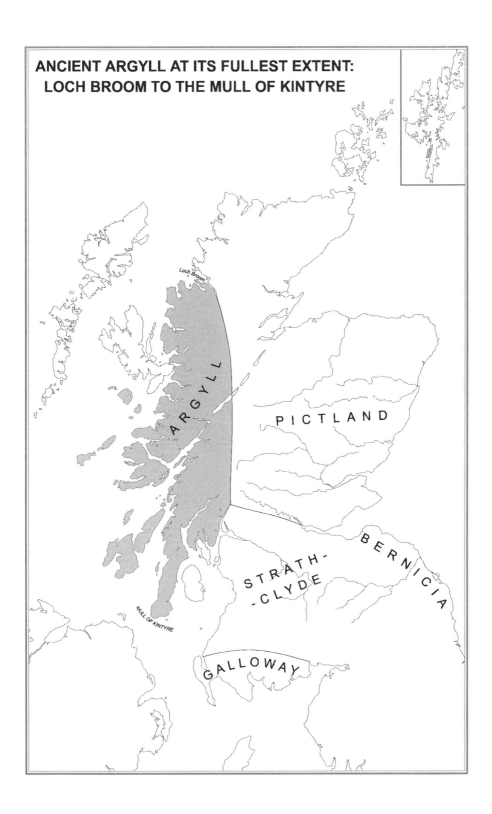

ANCIENT ARGYLL AT ITS FULLEST EXTENT:
LOCH BROOM TO THE MULL OF KINTYRE

Loch Broom

ARGYLL

PICTLAND

BERNICIA

STRATH-
-CLYDE

MULL OF KINTYRE

GALLOWAY

evidence of Irish (ie Scottish) settlements in Argyll. Gaelic words established in Scotland include district names in Argyll eg Kintyre, from Cinn-tìre, meaning headland or promontory; Cowal, from Còmghal, grandson of Fergus MacErc; Ben More, from Beinn Mhòr, meaning great mountain; Loch Loskin, from Loch Losgainn, meaning frog loch; Achaglachach, meaning field of little dells; Taynuilt, from Tigh an Uillt, meaning house of, or at, the stream.

In the year 329 the three Colla brothers – Colla Uais, Colla Dacrioch and Colla Meann arrived from Ireland. The history of the MacDonalds refers to the clan as Clan Cholla (the Clan of Colla), pointing back to this early period, and claims their descent from Colla Uais. He was definitely a historical person and seems to have been expelled, with his brothers, after a power struggle with Muireadhach Tireach, who seized the sovereignty of Ireland from him. There are many versions of this tale and, regardless of why Colla came to Scotland, the bards claimed that Somerled was descended from his eldest son, Eochaidh.

By 498, when the royal dynasty of Scots from Irish Dalriada in the person of Fergus Mòr, son of Erc, and his brothers, left Dunseverick, their Irish capital, and took up permanent residence in Scotland, it can be assumed that Scottish Dalriada was not only already well established as a colony, but was rapidly becoming more important than Irish Dalriada.

It is from this Irish culture, with its Gaelic Celtic language, that Scotland's identity originally sprang. Even the old name, 'Scotia', the Latin name for the land of the Scotti or Scots, as well as the usual 'Hibernia', was brought by the Irish immigrants to the new settlements in western Scotland, and this name was shared both by colony and mother country for some time, until it became associated with the colony alone. This Gaelic culture is increasingly recognised as being an important factor in the preservation of the identity of the nation. Originally, a Scot was known as a Gàidheal, or Gael, but nowadays that refers only to a native Gaelic-speaking Highlander. The population of Dalriada from this time onward continued to be largely Scoto-Irish.

It was in the ninth century that the Clan Cholla rose into greater consequence in Argyll and the Isles until their very existence was threatened by the Norsemen. Irish kings also were kept too busy fending off Norse attacks to indulge in any major aggression in Scotland.

In later years Somerled was to rely heavily upon Irish support to

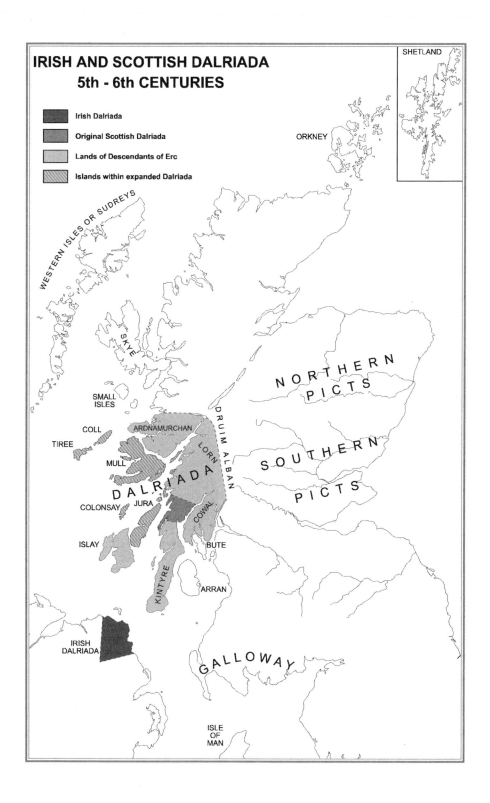

IRISH AND SCOTTISH DALRIADA
5th - 6th CENTURIES

Irish Dalriada

Original Scottish Dalriada

Lands of Descendants of Erc

Islands within expanded Dalriada

SHETLAND

ORKNEY

WESTERN ISLES OR SUDREYS

SKYE

NORTHERN PICTS

SOUTHERN PICTS

SMALL ISLES

COLL

TIREE

ARDNAMURCHAN

DRUIM ALBAN

LORN

MULL

DALRIADA

COLONSAY

JURA

COWAL

ISLAY

BUTE

KINTYRE

ARRAN

IRISH DALRIADA

GALLOWAY

ISLE OF MAN

regain his patrimony, and Irish mercenaries or gallow-glasses (gall-òglaich) in order to sustain his many campaigns, including the final, fatal expedition in 1164.

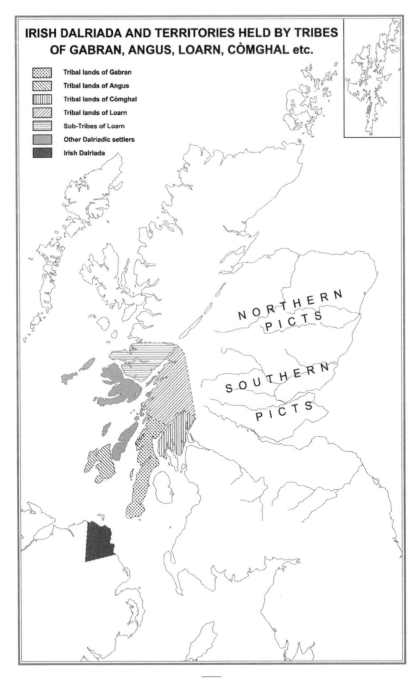

IRISH DALRIADA AND TERRITORIES HELD BY TRIBES OF GABRAN, ANGUS, LOARN, CÒMGHAL etc.

- Tribal lands of Gabran
- Tribal lands of Angus
- Tribal lands of Còmghal
- Tribal lands of Loarn
- Sub-Tribes of Loarn
- Other Dalriadic settlers
- Irish Dalriada

NORTHERN PICTS

SOUTHERN PICTS

CHAPTER EIGHT

Lords of Galloway

The original seven ancient Celtic kingdoms of Scotland, each under the control of its Rì, are listed in *De Situ Albanie*, Skene's *Picts and Scots*, and by Bishop Andrew of Caithness in the Introduction to *Early Sources of Scottish History*. Galloway is not included in either account but it was, undoubtedly, an ancient sub-kingdom, a semi-independent province ruled by men calling themselves, variously, 'king' or 'regulus', 'prince', 'earl' and 'lord'. The population was originally Celtic with an English overlay but, according to the *Annals of Ulster*, it is possible that there were Gall-Gàidheil there in the mid-ninth century. In the early tenth century many Norwegians appear to have left Ireland, and some settled in Scotland, including Galloway, as there was a partial cessation of war between the Irish and the Norwegians from 877 to 914. By the mid-tenth century Cumbria was known as a stepping stone between the Norwegians of Ireland, Wales and Galloway, and the Danes of Northumbria, showing a substantial Norse presence across Britain.

By the early twelfth century Fergus was Lord of Galloway, and he comes into the story of Somerled as a wild card in the complicated game of politics in the western islands. According to the *Chronicle of Man*, Olaf the Red, King of Man, took as his second wife, Affrica, Fergus' daughter, by whom he had a son, Godred or Godfrey – later king of Man after his father. She was not, however, the mother of Ragnhildis, or Ragnhilde, Somerled's wife, but the stepmother.

This marriage was probably arranged in accordance with Olaf's policy of making friends with people who could possibly be a threat to him, and Fergus, the ally of Man was infinitely preferable to Fergus, the enemy of Man. Fergus was cunningly dangerous and not to be trusted, but he had a notable fleet which, allied with that of Olaf, was a powerful force for those who strove to control the western seas.

In addition the Galloway kerns were an uncontrollable and vicious band of thugs, every bit as bad as the Norsemen. Having them as allies was a doubtful blessing, as they could prove to be a complete liability rather than an asset.

CHAPTER NINE

Dublin Norse

Somerled always had to consider the possible alliance against himself of the Dublin Norse, along with Man, England, Galloway, Orkney or Norway. Certainly the Dubliners were not major players in the game, but their very presence provided uncertainty as to where they would give their unpredictable support – and the service of their invaluable fleets – thereby helping to tip the balance of power in the Hebrides, one way or the other.

Like Man, Norse Dublin was, nominally at least, under Norwegian suzerainty, the Norsemen having originally come to Ireland during the first waves of attacks around the year 794. The *Annals of Ulster* tell of the devastation of the whole of Britain by the Vikings, and that the Isle of Rathlin, off the north Antrim coast, was burned in 795. The *Annals of Innisfallen* tell of the attacks on Ireland by the 'gentiles' in 796, and again the *Annals of Ulster* report attacks in 798 when Ireland was attacked and burned, and serious incursions were made both in Scotland and Ireland. The words 'Danes' and 'Scandinavians' are often used, as well as 'gentiles' and 'foreigners', but the invaders would seem to have been mainly Norwegian. There was continual warfare among the Norse, the Dalriads, the Orcadians, the Picts, the Gall-Gàidheil and the Irish, but soon settlements began to be made, and held, even in the midst of conflict, and the Norse built harbours and cities, including Dublin, and engaged in trade.

Harald Fairhair's Saga, states that Thorgils and Frodi founded Dublin, but the *Annals of Ulster* disagree, saying that the Norwegians built a castle in Dublin in 841, twenty years after their first recorded invasion of the district.

Other sources refer to the settlement of the Norsemen in Ireland and some blame the indolence of the Irish for allowing the newcomers to seize the land and, later, the trade:

Giraldus Cambrensis, in his *Topographia Hibernica*, describes how, in the year 850, some Norsemen came to Ireland, presenting themselves as traders. The Irish, described as too indolent to be bothered going abroad themselves in order to trade, allowed the Norse, gradually, to establish themselves in Irish ports, bringing their valuable goods with them, and building trading posts around the coasts, with the full compliance of the local chiefs. The Norsemen, literally, dug themselves in, establishing new settlements and then towns, without having to lift a sword to do so and, as a bonus, taking lucrative trade from right under the noses of the Irish.

Inevitably the growth of the prosperous trading centre of Dublin attracted the unwelcome attention of other Norsemen, and there was constant terrorism, with Black-Gentile Vikings fighting White-Gentile Vikings over the spoils, until the king of Norway's son plundered the town in 853 and forced the Irish to pay tribute to him. From now onwards the Norse were well established in Dublin, from where they set out on raids of piracy into Strathclyde and England, bringing back plunder and slaves.

The Irish, however, did not give in without a fight, and *Nial's Saga*, tells of the Battle of Clontarf, in 1014, which decided whether Ireland would be ruled by its own High King, or by the Scandinavians.

The Norse had gathered supporters from far and wide, and certainly had with them pure Norse forces under Sitric (or Sigtrygg) King of Dublin, and Sigurd, Earl of Orkney, as well as pro-Norse Gall-Gàidheal islanders, and men from mainland Argyll including Kintyre. The Irish were led by Brian Boraimhe, High King of Ireland. Some Irish fought alongside the Norse, fearing the power of Boraimhe, whose death in this battle was to give rise to dynastic turbulence and political infighting in which some Viking chiefs offered their services to first one Irish king and then another. Their usefulness to the Irish lay in their fleets and thereby their control of the seaways.

The battle was fiercely long and destructive but resulted in the overwhelming victory of the Irish, although Boraimhe was killed. The Norse losses were very heavy and included Earl Sigurd. They were now confined to the Dublin district, and no longer a threat to Ireland as a whole, though conflict broke out between the Irish and the Norse on many subsequent occasions.

For a while the Viking settlement of Dublin was part of the Kingdom of Man. In 1075 Godred Crovan, son of Magnus the Black of Iceland, collected a large fleet of ships and attacked Man, whose King, Godfrey Sigtryggsson or MacSitric, had sheltered him after the

Norse defeat at Stamford Bridge (see chapter 3). The *Chronicle of Man* tells us that, in addition, Crovan also captured Dublin and part of Leinster.

During the reign of Magnus Bareleg there was continual conflict between the Dublin Norse and the Irish, before the king made three expeditions 'west over sea' to subdue the Kingdom of Man and the Hebrides, in 1093, 1098 and 1102-3. The exact details of each raid are unclear, but Magnus made punitive raids on all parts of his unruly territories, including Ireland, and it appears that Dublin was a battle-ground in 1102. The *Annals of the Four Masters* report that there was a military expedition of the Irish against Magnus and his Vikings, who had come on a plundering raid to Dublin – and the *Heimskringla*, Magnus Bareleg's Saga, tell us that Dublin was captured and taken into the control of Magnus.

After the death of Magnus, bands of Dublin Norse pirates rampaged uncontrolled throughout the west, fighting for loot, slaves, food, and so on, and caring nothing for lands or ideas of glory, each group more or less self-contained, and jealous over the control of its own area. Somerled was always concerned for the security of the Clyde islands of Arran and Bute, whose coasts were dominated by Norse pirate bands as, in the wrong hands, they constituted a threat to Kintyre and indeed to the whole of Argyll.

In 1154 the Dublin Norse leaders, in the persons of the three nephews of Olaf Bitling, king of Man and the Isles, demanded of their elderly uncle that half of the kingdom should be given to them. Having tricked Olaf into meeting them at Ramsey harbour, one nephew, Ronald, murdered his uncle and thereby brought down upon the islanders the very strife that Olaf had worked so shrewdly to avoid for all the years of his reign, and divided the land up among themselves. But Godred the Black, Olaf's son, regained his father's kingdom the following year.

CHAPTER TEN

Earls of Orkney

Tryst of a fleet against Castle Sween
Welcome is the adventure in Ireland
Norsemen travelling the billows
Brown barks are being cleaned for them.
Tall men are arraying the fleet
Which swiftly holds its course on the sea's bare surface
No hand lacks a trim warspear
In battle of targes, polished and comely.
Of quilted hauberks is arrayed
The bark's forefront in form of jewels
Of warriors with brown-faced girdles
They are Norsemen and nobles.

A GAELIC POEM OF AROUND 1310

During the Viking era it is difficult to keep track of who was in control of the western seaboard from one year to the next. Suzerainty was contested by the kings of Norway, Man, Dublin, Dalriada and the earls of Orkney, at different times.

The earls of Orkney were under the suzerainty of the kings of Norway and, like the Norse of Dublin, were unpredictable, and therefore worth watching, being potentially dangerous through their ownership of well-built and well-maintained fleets of longships. This gave them control over the Innse-Gall as well as their own Northern Isles. At any given time the state of relations between the Orkneys and Norway was of great interest to Somerled.

There is evidence of very early racial fusion between the Norwegians and the earlier Celtic inhabitants of the Northern and Western Isles, according to the *Annals of the Four Masters*. This brought the Norsemen right into what was to be Somerled's 'back yard', and although the Orkney earls were always the far from obedient servants of the Norwegian kings, as evidence from the wild tales of the *Orkneyinga Saga* proves, yet there was an undeniable, and more or less unbroken, contact between the Northern Isles and Norway for eight hundred years, and a potential Norway-Orkney alliance was always a powerful threat to the rest of the Isles.

Prudentius of Troyes tells how the Scots, after being harassed by the Norse for many years, were finally overwhelmed, and the Norse forcibly took possession of the Orkney group of islands, thus describing how the Orkney islands first came into the possession of the Crown of Norway, though the mainland territories of Caithness and Sutherland belonged, nominally, to the Scottish Crown. But it has to be said that, right from the days of King Harald Fairhair's oppression of his fellow countrymen, the Norse of the islands tried to maintain their autonomy from the Norwegian kings – with varying degrees of success.

Generations of Scottish kings were well aware of, and very interested in, what went on in the north of their kingdom, but had neither the time, the inclination, nor the power, to do anything about the state of affairs offshore, thus leaving the Orkney earls the freedom to entrench themselves in the area.

The indigenous Celtic peoples, therefore, had no High King to appeal to for protection against the blight of piracy and later, of land grabbing. In the early twelfth century Somerled must have appeared to them as the White Knight galloping to the rescue, though he was ultimately unsuccessful as regards controlling the Nordreys during his own lifetime.

Gretti's Saga, as well as the *Heimskringla*, would seem to suggest that the original settlements in Orkney and Shetland (the Nordreys) were an obvious result of Harald Fairhair's reprisals after the Battle of Hafrsfiordr, around the year 872, after which he became sole ruler of Norway. But, apart from providing sanctuary, the Nordreys gradually assumed a great deal of importance simply because of their geographical position. They became bases from which to strike at the northern and western mainland of Scotland, all the western islands down to Man, Anglesey and the west coast of Wales, and Ireland itself – all of which were extensively raided from about 800.

Although the Orkneys sat amidst formidable sea hazards, such as rip tides, currents, whirlpools, skerries, reefs and overfalls, the anchorages were a magnet to good seamen, and the open, sandy beaches ideal for beaching ships. They were well placed on the major sea routes between Norway and the Hebrides, Man and Dublin. The Norse colonists soon came to appreciate and enjoy the riches now available to them through trade with all the lands within range of their longships. They would fight fiercely for the privilege of keeping this position. Somerled never did manage to get control of the Orkneys – despite his mastery of the western seas right up to the northernmost Hebrides, by the mid-twelfth century.

Orkney was also a focus for the Norse settlers in Caithness and Sutherland who, not wishing to draw the attention of Norwegian or Scottish kings down upon themselves, used Orkney as a power base instead of their former homeland of Norway. The earldom reached its zenith in the eleventh century in the days of the famous Earl Thornfinn the Mighty. In the later years of his life Thorfinn became a professed Christian and established an Episcopal church at Birsay and the first bishopric in Scandinavia with, as its first bishop, Thorolf, who helped him to restructure the government of his earldom. Thorfinn ruled with wise autonomy, although nominally subject to the kings of both Norway and Scotland, and raised the status of the Orkneys to a high point which they have never again achieved.

During Malcolm III's reign the earldom of Orkney was undisturbed by the Scottish king who was regularly engaged in campaigns in northern England.

Earl Thorfinn lived until 1065, and by that time had control of nine earldoms, all of the Hebrides and part of Ireland, though Norse penetration of mainland Scotland was confined to coastal areas and not deep inland because of resistance from the Picts who could always retreat into the higher ground and impenetrable glens of the north from where they were able to launch guerrilla attacks on the interlopers. There was, therefore, little commerce or intermarriage between Picts and Norse, so nothing resembling the Gall-Gàidheil situation existed in the northern mainland.

Throughout Somerled's era and beyond, the Norse ruled these areas with minimal interference from Norway and Scotland. This was the high-water mark of the power and prestige of the Orcadian earldom.

In Somerled's time however, there was fear that King Sigurd (Crusader) of Norway might attempt to gather up all the mainland and island territories held by Norsemen into one united Norse empire under his sway. The resources of Orkney would be invaluable in this project, and in particular Orkney's fleet would cause Somerled considerable problems in patrolling his scattered island kingdom's vast sea area, and defending it from attack. Only when Somerled became lord of Skye about 1150, and cleared that large island of Vikings, was the Norse, and in particular, Orkney, presence eliminated on the entire Hebridean seaboard for the time being. Skye had been a thorn in the Lordship's side, being a convenient base for piracy by the Orkneymen and men of Innse-Gall.

Somerled wanted the Outer Hebrides to remain right out of Orkney control, especially as an alliance between Norway, Orkney, and Godred the Black of Man (his brother-in-law), would be a powerful threat to his Isles kingdom. Consolidation of his rule over the Inner and Outer Hebrides would be a bulwark against this threat.

After Somerled's time the line of the Norse Orkney Earls ended in 1231 with the death of Earl Harald's son, John, and the succession of Scottish Earls of Orkney followed. The failure of King Hakon's 1263 expedition marked the beginning of the Nordreys' gradual isolation from Norway, until 1468 when Orkney was sold to the Scottish Crown for 50,000 Rhenish florins, and 1469, Shetland, for 8,000 florins.

PART TWO

The Kingdom of Argyll and the Isles

CHAPTER ELEVEN

Somerled's Ancestry
and Claim to Argyll

Who exactly was this man, Somerled, what were his origins and by what right did he claim the lordship of Argyll? These are questions which have exercised the minds of historians past and present.

There are wide ranging arguments for and against Somerled's ancestry being possibly Pictish, Scots, Irish or Gall-Gàidheal, but he is generally assumed to be of Scots-Irish extraction.

The Clan Donald historians The Rev A MacDonald (Killearnan) and The Rev A MacDonald (Kiltarlity), writing in 1896, name him definitely as the founder of the Family of the Isles, subsequently known as the Clan Donald or MacDonald, and name him Somerled Rex Insularum, Somerled King of the Isles. Despite his undoubtedly Norse name – Somerled, or Summer Sailor, which he may have been given by a possibly Norse mother – the MacDonalds claim that there is not a shred of evidence of Norse descent in the male line. They also refer to the spirit and tendency of the House of Somerled being in direct antagonism to the Norwegian occupation of the west of Scotland. They insist that if Somerled had been a Norseman he'd hardly have spent his entire life trying to throw the Norse out of Scotland and impose an alien Gaelic culture in their place. It seems that The Rev A and A MacDonald presume Somerled to be a man of highly honourable principles, as a mere pirate would scarcely care about the supremacy of his race and would go his own way regardless, as many of the Norse and Gall-Gàidheil Vikings certainly did. But then the authors are MacDonalds, and no doubt biased in favour of the ancestral hero of their clan.

They also point out that the title Rìgh-Fhiongall, commonly used by MacDonald chiefs, is no proof in itself of Norse descent as, after Somerled, the Lords of the Isles ruled over a large extent of the territory which, in former times, had been subject to the kings of Man to whom

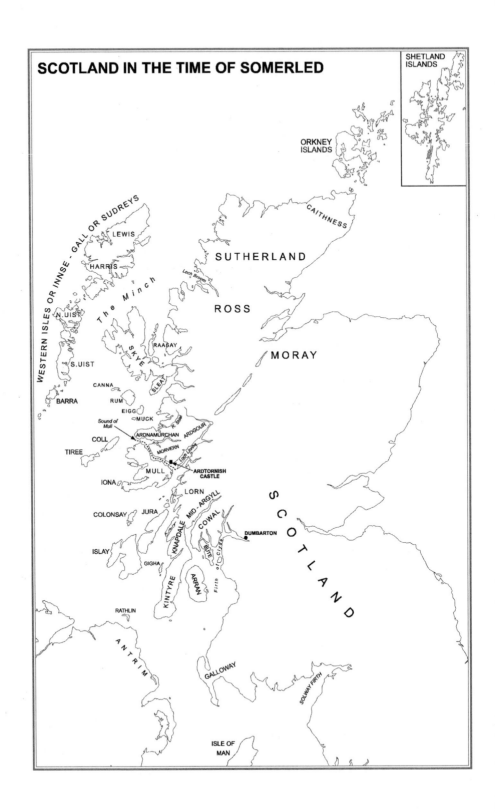

SCOTLAND IN THE TIME OF SOMERLED

SHETLAND ISLANDS

ORKNEY ISLANDS

CAITHNESS

SUTHERLAND

ROSS

MORAY

LEWIS

HARRIS

Loch Broom

The Minch

N. UIST

S. UIST

SKYE

RAASAY

SLEAT

CANNA

RUM

EIGG

MUCK

Sound of Mull

ARDNAMURCHAN

ARDGOUR

MORVERN

R. Shiel

Loch Linnhe

BARRA

COLL

TIREE

MULL

ARDTORNISH CASTLE

IONA

LORN

COLONSAY

JURA

MID - ARGYLL

COWAL

KNAPDALE

BUTE

SCOTLAND

DUMBARTON

ISLAY

GIGHA

KINTYRE

ARRAN

Firth of Clyde

RATHLIN

A N T R I M

GALLOWAY

SOLWAY FIRTH

ISLE OF MAN

WESTERN ISLES OR INNSE - GALL OR SUDREYS

this royal designation had been originally applied.

Having decided that Somerled was not of Norse origin they dispose of the argument about whether he was of Pictish or Scottish descent by saying that it is a somewhat subordinate one, seeing that both these nations emerged from the same root stock: offshoots of the Gaelic and British branches of the Celtic tree.

In deciding which branch to favour they quote contemporary authors. Dr WF Skene's *The Highlanders of Scotland* strongly supports the theory of Somerled's Pictish descent. He maintains that the Gàidheil of Argyll who were later known, he says, as the Gall-Gàidheil, were of Pictish stock, and that Somerled's ancestors were of the Gall-Gàidheil, according to family evidence and historical sources from the *Orkneyinga Saga*.

He was not consistent in his view in this matter, as, in his 1862 Introduction to the sixteenth century *Book of the Dean of Lismore* he seems to contradict himself by saying that the origins of the Clan Donald were undoubtedly Irish Celtic, and the names of Somerled's paternal ancestors obviously were too. The whole tone of the family's activities was to drive out the Norse who had invaded their traditional territories, and to re-instate the Gaels in their rightful place. This could be done only with Irish support, especially Irish family support.

The Clan Donald historians oppose Dr Skene's support for his original Gall-Gàidheal theory and state that the Dalriadic Scots had occupied Argyll for centuries before King Kenneth MacAlpin united the Scots and the Picts into one kingdom, and they were undoubtedly the dominant race in the west. They find it absurd to suggest that the Dalriads would suddenly just arise and go from Dalriada between the ninth and eleventh centuries. They utterly refute the idea that Somerled was of the Gall-Gàidheil, saying that the despised Gall-Gàidheil were little more than pirates with no emotional attachment to the lands they lived in, whereas Somerled's Clan Donald had centuries of occupation of their tribal lands behind them, and were of traditional Dalriadic stock with strongly forged links between their original heartland of Ireland, and Argyll and its isles.

The establishment of the Gaelic kingdom was largely promoted by Irish aid; matrimonial alliances with Irish families were frequently formed by the chiefs; many members of these families acquired settlements in Antrim and Tyrone, and the bards and seannachies (story-tellers and genealogists) of the Isles went for their education to the literary schools of the North of Ireland. All these circumstances seem to point to the same conclusion.

Another contemporary historian of the MacDonald ministers was Donald Gregory, who published his *History of the Western Highlands and Islands of Scotland* in 1881. His comments on Somerled's ancestry were dismissed curtly by them, and they gave their opinion that Gregory seemed to dodge the issue of a Celtic or Norse origin, never mind the more precise one of a Pictish versus a Scots-Irish descent.

Gregory, like the Clan Donald historians, also says that Somerled was the undoubted founder of the Clan Donald Lords of the Isles, but admitted that his origin was quite obscure. He, too, notes that Somerled's name was Norse, and that his father's and grandfather's were Celtic, but says that it is impossible to found any argument on the Christian names alone. He continues that, according to Irish and Highland seannachies, Gilleadamnan was sixth in descent from Godfrey MacFergus, Toiseach (military leader) of the Isles, and that, in 836 Godfrey MacFergus, lord of Oriel (counties Monaghan and Louth in Eire and county Armagh in Northern Ireland) was asked by Kenneth MacAlpin to come over to Scotland to help him establish control of Dalriada. It seems that Kenneth then rewarded Godfrey with grants of land in Dalriada.

Gregory also refers to the manuscript *History of the MacDonalds* by Hugh MacDonald, a seannachie from Sleat, Skye, writing in 1680, who says that this Godfrey was expelled from the Argyll territories granted to him by the grateful Kenneth during Harald Fairhair's conquest of the Isles. Godfrey was reputed to have descended from the alternative line of Fergus MacErc, who had two sons, Domangart and Godfrey. The former succeeded his father, and was the progenitor of Kenneth MacAlpin, and succeeding Scottish kings, and Godfrey, the younger son, is claimed to be the progenitor, through Godfrey MacFergus, of the line from which Somerled and the Clan Donald sprang. Gregory says that Celtic genealogists trace Godfrey MacFergus' line back to Conn Cheud Chath, the famous High King of Ireland, who reigned from 177-212 AD, thus maintaining that Somerled was of Scots-Irish descent. This is probably more clearly seen in the genealogical table on the page opposite.

Gregory then goes on to accede that Somerled's name was obviously Norse, and that many people claim that he was a Scandinavian by descent in the male line. He says that Somerled was mentioned in the

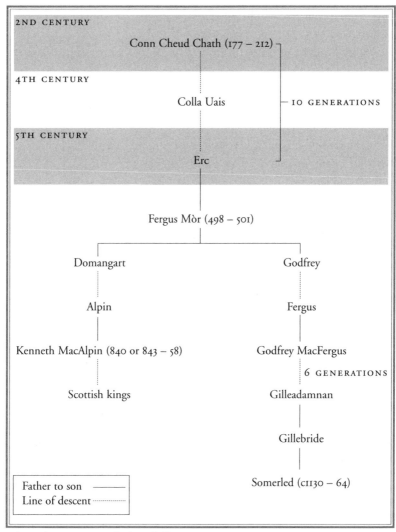

The Irish connection and Clan Cholla.

Norse Sagas, but not in such a way as to definitely indicate his origin. He is referred to as Sumerlidi 'Haulldr' (a cultivator of the soil and not of noble birth – but 'Haulldr' was a common nickname among kings and nobles, so no inference about Somerled's rank can be drawn from the use of this word here). Gregory feels that the tone of the Saga references is rather against Somerled being considered a Norseman, though the reference to a noted ancestor named Godfrey may be to Gofra, or Godfrey MacArailt, King of the Isles, who died in 989.

However, Gregory concludes that four-hundred-year-old Highland

and Irish tradition would seem to support Somerled's Scots-Irish pedigree.

More modern supporters of the theory of Somerled's Celtic origins are Dr IF Grant in *The Lordship of the Isles*, 1982, and John Bannerman in *Who Are The Scots?* 1971.

John Bannerman is definite in his assertion of Somerled's Scoto-Irish Celtic ancestry, and refers to Godfrey MacFergus as an important member of the Airgialla, a people subordinated to the Cenèl Loairn (tribe of Lorn; see maps in Part One). They were of the Northern Irish Uí Macc-Uais family, some of whom had settled in the Scottish Dalriadic islands controlled by the Cenèl Loairn, in a vassal relationship. When the power and influence of the Cenèl Loairn, and its rival the Cenèl Gabrain, had been weakened by internal strife and Pictish aggression in the early eighth century, Godfrey MacFergus, apparently a member of the ruling family of the Airgialla, gave assistance to Kenneth MacAlpin in helping to control Dalriada, and thereafter settled in that area. From him is descended Somerled, King of Argyll, whose descendants became the Lords of the Isles.

IF Grant is another modern proponent of Somerled's Celtic pedigree, and, in her chapter on Somerled, says that the fact that he had a Norse name does not detract from the centuries of tradition that he was the descendant of Conn and Colla Uais, two of the most renowned Irishmen in history. It was of this ancient, royal descent that MacVurich, the bard, reminded the Clan before the Battle of Harlaw, in 1411, in order to arouse their fighting spirit:

A Chlanna Chuinn cuimhnichibh
Cruas an am na h-iorghuill

(Remember, Children of Conn
The hardiehood of the time of battles)

She continues, in assertive vein: 'Colla Uais – is an historical personage, and his descent from Conn may be considered as proven. There are several genealogies that deal with the descent from Colla Uais to Somerled. One is a manuscript of 1450; one is contained in the sixteenth century collections made by the Dean of Lismore; one is recorded by the MacDonald seannachie in the seventeenth century, and five are Irish. They are all closely similar – none of them can be complete for only about a dozen individual lives have to cover the period of over six hundred years between Colla Uais and Somerled – Fergus and his son Godfrey appear, and the latter may be the same as the "Godfrey, Fergus's son, Lord of the Hebrides" who died in 853 according to the *Annals of the Four Masters*.'

RL Bremner, putting forward a different point of view, in *The Norsemen in Alban,* 1923, supports the view that Somerled was of Gall-Gàidheal stock and, like the others, notes his Norse name, and his father's and grandfather's Celtic names. He puts this down to the fact that the population of the mainland coast from Kintyre to Cape Wrath, and the islands, had been intermingled Celt and Norse for three centuries before Somerled and says that there can be no doubt at all that Somerled, who had married a Norse woman, and had given two of his sons Norse names, was himself of mixed blood, ie Gall-Gàidheal. He makes no mention of any Scoto-Irish connection, but mentions as an early ancestor of Somerled, Sigurd the Stout, Earl of Orkney (950–1014), whose son Thorfinn became Earl after him, and whose daughter married Earl Gilli, by name a Norseman. He continues that on the death of Earl Sigurd and during the minority of Thorfinn, Earl Gilli must have been the supreme ruler of the Sudreys, and refers, from the *Annals of the Four Masters,* to the death in 1083 of Somerled, son of King Gillibrigid of the Sudreys or Innsegall He gives, as Somerled's family tree:

Earl Gilli (-brigid), King of Innsigall

Somerled

Gilli-Adomnan

Gilli-brigid

Somerled

Bremner says that the family's loss of their ancestral lands happened much later than is generally thought by the other writers, basing this idea on tales by the seannachies of how the Norwegians and other Vikings drove Somerled's grandfather out of his ancestral lands, to seek sanctuary in Ireland.

He states that this is either a resumption by the Norse kings of Man of their island realm after the death of Thorfinn or a result of the attacks by Magnus Bareleg in 1093 and 1098.

D MacEacharna, a modern author, and an Islayman, writing from the island in *The Lands of the Lordship* in 1976, writes briefly and rather dismissively about Somerled, giving him a wholly Norse ancestry, having a Norse name which was fairly unusual in the Hebrides. He refers to the marriage of Somerled to Ragnhildis, daughter of Olaf (The Red/Bitling/Morsel), King of Man and the Isles and notes that from this marriage were descended the famous MacDonald and MacDougall clans, as well as some less well known. MacEacharna pokes rather sarcastic fun at the MacDonald historians by saying that it was unthinkable to Clan Donald that these two great clans could possibly be Norse and not Scottish in origin: Something had to be done about it. And so he accuses them of having cooked up a fine story of Somerled – admittedly Norse by name – and his Gaelic-named father Gille-bride, both having been a thorn in the side of the Norse while trying to regain control of the Isles. MacEacharna then continues disparagingly that careless modern historians have ignored the fact that the Norse King Olaf the Red was unlikely to have accepted into his family an anti-Norse son-in-law, in the person of Somerled, who did nothing towards bringing the Isles safely into the kingdom of Scotland, but foolishly declared war on that kingdom and threw his life away on a stupid adventure in Renfrewshire – rather a simplistic account of the complicated and momentous events of 1130–64. However, this author is entitled to his opinion though it is a minority one emanating, surprisingly, from a MacDonald island.

The majority, pro-Celtic view, seems to explain the motivation for Somerled's hard-fought campaigns in the west, with continual Irish support, right up to the final battle in 1164.

CHAPTER TWELVE

Rise of Somerled

The actual appearance of Somerled as a young man took place about 1130 according to local tradition, in Morvern, the Argyll district most closely associated with his family. It was to become one of the most valuable possessions of the Lords of the Isles, and Ardtornish Castle, in the Sound of Mull, was to become closely associated with the events of the fledgling kingdom.

The Clan Donald historians paint a gloomy picture of crisis in Somerled's family fortunes at this time. His grandfather, Gilleadamnan, had been driven from his considerable Argyll lands by the Norse (probably King Harald Fairhair) and had sought refuge in County Fermanagh, with his kindred of Clan Cholla. In addition, Somerled's father Gillebride had made a series of unsuccessful forays, with Fermanagh help, on the Morvern and Ardgour districts of Argyll in an attempt to dislodge the Norse invaders, but the latter had such a hold on the entire west coast by this time that all the islands from Man to the Orkneys, and the coastlands from Dumbarton to Caithness, were in their possession.

Eventually Gillebride and his men were forced to hide in the woods and caves of Morvern, from where they carried out sporadic, and largely ineffectual, guerrilla attacks on the enemy. Gillebride was becoming known as Gillebride na h-Uaimh (Gillebride of the Cave) – hardly an inspiring title for a war leader. The family's fortunes seemed to be at their lowest ebb. The Norse were poised to drive them, finally, out of the Isles and completely destroy their authority in mainland Argyll itself.

It was at this point that Gillebride was displaced in the leadership by his son Somerled, an inspiring personality and impressive natural tactician who was not only eventually to regain the family possessions, but also to add significantly to them, and to raise the family name to royal status. Initially the odds seemed stacked against him – his father a broken reed, the Norse apparently immovably entrenched, few supporters available, apart from the Fermanagh men, and his family name humiliated by the manner of its downfall at the hands of the usurpers.

The actual events of Somerled's early life are shrouded in the mists of unverifiable folktales, but Clan tradition describes him as being of middle height, good-looking, with pleasant but piercing eyes, good tempered and very intelligent. His personality is described as authoritative and impressive, with great force of character, fuelled by extraordinary energy and ambition, but yet perceptive and wise in his military and political decisions – traits essential in a ruler and leader of men. Subsequent events were fully to justify this glowing approbation, albeit a partisan one by members of the Clan.

As might be expected, Somerled's first foray into military leadership involved a last desperate attempt by certain Argyll clans to prevent what seemed the inevitable, decisive blow by the Norsemen for supremacy in Argyll.

The Norse longships swarmed into the western seas and their forces fiercely attacked the coasts of Argyll, pushing back and crushing all opposition by the native clans. However, Somerled was identified as the impressive young warrior who had retaliated ferociously against the attackers, while leading the MacInneses of Morvern, after their own chief had been killed in the battle. He was named as Somhairle Mòr MacGhillebhride – Somerled the Mighty, son of Gillebride.

According to this heroic legend an aged chief of the Clan MacInnes then recommended Somerled as their new leader as one who, from his prowess in the recent conflict, was well-fitted for such a post. The suggestion was unanimously approved, and Somerled was asked to take command.

In this legendary tale, however, Somerled seems to have been initially rather hesitant about taking on such a responsibility in view of the obvious strength of the opposition, but having finally accepted the leadership he came up with the kind of stratagem of the instinctive guerrilla fighter. Hugh MacDonald, the Sleat historian, gives a fanciful version of the story in his 1680 manuscript and tells of how, when Somerled joined the MacInneses, he saw that they were greatly outnumbered by the Norsemen. Having instructed them to kill a herd of grazing cows, and to skin them, he ordered his little group to march around the hill on which they were gathered, then to put on the cowhides to disguise themselves, and repeat the action. Finally he

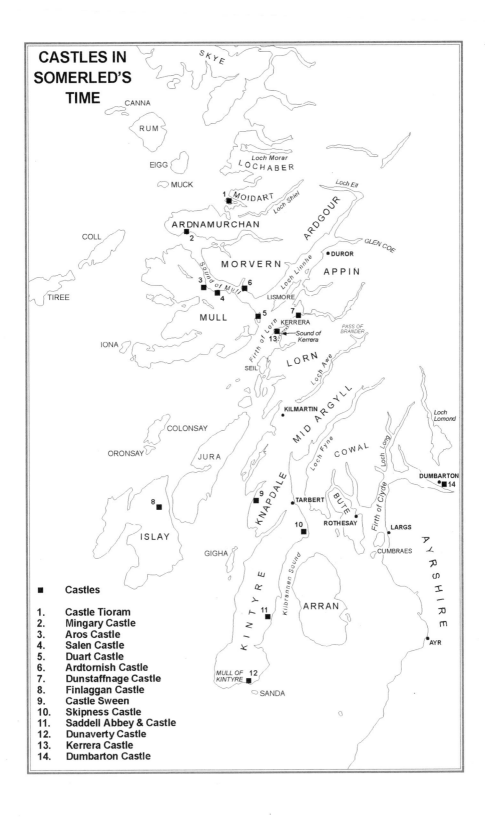

CASTLES IN SOMERLED'S TIME

SKYE

CANNA

RUM

EIGG

MUCK

Loch Morar

LOCHABER

1 MOIDART

Loch Shiel

Loch Eil

ARDGOUR

ARDNAMURCHAN

2

COLL

MORVERN

Loch Linnhe

GLEN COE

DUROR

APPIN

3

6

Sound of Mull

TIREE

4

LISMORE

5

7

KERRERA

PASS OF BRANDER

MULL

13

Sound of Kerrera

Firth of Lorn

IONA

SEIL

LORN

Loch Awe

COLONSAY

KILMARTIN

MID ARGYLL

Loch Lomond

ORONSAY

JURA

Loch Fyne

COWAL

Loch Long

DUMBARTON

14

9

KNAPDALE

TARBERT

BUTE

Firth of Clyde

LARGS

8

10

ROTHESAY

CUMBRAES

AYRSHIRE

ISLAY

GIGHA

Kilbrannan Sound

KINTYRE

11

ARRAN

AYR

MULL OF KINTYRE

12

SANDA

■ **Castles**

1. **Castle Tioram**
2. **Mingary Castle**
3. **Aros Castle**
4. **Salen Castle**
5. **Duart Castle**
6. **Ardtornish Castle**
7. **Dunstaffnage Castle**
8. **Finlaggan Castle**
9. **Castle Sween**
10. **Skipness Castle**
11. **Saddell Abbey & Castle**
12. **Dunaverty Castle**
13. **Kerrera Castle**
14. **Dumbarton Castle**

ordered his men to reverse the cowhides and go round the hill a third time, in order to appear to the enemy as a strong force composed of three parts. According to the *Book of Clanranald*, Somerled then attacked the Norse force and drove them northwards to the River Shiel, where some were hunted down and killed, and the remainder escaped across with their leader and fled to the Isles.

It seems that Somerled's name was now made, and he became the focus for the resistance movement against the Norse in the west. His initial success no doubt gave heart to other dispossessed Gaels, who flocked to join him. Success breeds success and the clans took heart again.

There is no doubt that he was the man for the moment, instinctively knowing that this was his time, and following the commands of destiny towards the great position which he later achieved. He knew he had to press his advantage and continue attacking the Norsemen in their own strongholds, never letting up or allowing them any opportunity to regroup, or make alliances with one another. Men rallied to him, gaining confidence as their numbers grew, and a series of successful attacks was eventually to drive the Norsemen out of Argyll altogether – back as far as their bases in the Western Isles. The significance of this cannot be underestimated. This was the first time the Norwegians had met someone who dared to challenge their very presence in the western seas.

CHAPTER THIRTEEN

Building the Kingdom

From then onwards Somerled's story was one of an inexorable rise to power, using the tools available to him. There is surely no doubt that his reputation for invincibility must have been growing. His powerful personality and proven ability aroused the spirits of the Celtic people downtrodden by generations of Norse aggression.

The people who manned his forces, ships and castles were, firstly, remnants of his father's Fermanagh and Morvern forces and, increasingly, men from Ardgour, Lorn, Appin, Knapdale and Kintyre – all parts of his gradually recaptured Argyll – who thronged to join the charismatic young leader. As an ancient historian put it, these lands were his by right, as formerly belonging to and possessed by his predecessors. Right and might together make a formidable combination. Whether this is historically accurate or not, the likelihood is that it was close to the truth.

His right to raise men came from the ancient land system of Celtic nations, which was tribal and patriarchal. Celtic vassals owed allegiance to their chief as the head of the race, and not as the owner of the land, as in the feudal system. The word 'clan' itself, from the Gaelic 'clann', meaning 'children', emphasises the family structure of the system. The chief's duty was to protect and defend his people from the incursions of their enemies in peace or war and to do this he had the power to raise men. The chiefs encouraged all warlike skills including archery at which the Islesmen were acknowledged experts.

Later events during this momentous time were to bring in the Irish again, also the allied Manx and Galwegians with their Gaelic and Norse components; Gall-Gàidheil from Innse-Gall; Dublin Norse (occasional allies of the Manx) and Gaels from Moray and Ross (Somerled's brother-in-law was Malcolm, Earl of Ross). This unlikely mix threw in their lot with Somerled for their own good reasons, which were to become evident in the fullness of time.

Also, very importantly, Somerled was acquiring an intimate

knowledge of the complicated geography of the west, which could be used to his advantage. The restored Ardtornish Castle, on its rock near the junction of Loch Aline with the Sound of Mull, was the hub of a wheel of seaways giving access to the mainland Argyll districts of Lorn, Appin and Lochaber to the east; to north-east Mull; and to Moidart and Sunart in the west and north, as well as controlling Morvern and Ardgour. The spokes of the wheel were the Sound of Mull itself, the Firth of Lorn, the Sound of Kerrera and the large sea lochs of Linnhe, Creran and Etive. Whoever held this strategic area controlled the main routes to the Inner and Outer Hebrides, and much of the jagged and

Right. Castle Sween.
11th century Norman-style keep
with later additions.

Below. Castle Tioram, Moidart.
The northernmost of Somerled's
castles.

Bottom. Dunaverty Rock. Site of
Dunaverty Castle, probably the
southernmost.

indented mainland coast so favoured by Viking raiders. These seaways, sheltered from the open Atlantic, provided reasonably secure routes through the tide races, currents, reefs, skerries and whirlpools which are such a hazardous feature of the west coast of Scotland, and gave Somerled the power to strike often and fast at the pockets of Norsemen who had dominated these same seaways before his arrival.

The Norse were known as among the fiercest fighters in the world and were increasingly prevalent all round the coast, but the fact that there was often bad blood between the various gangs was an advantage to Somerled.

They therefore had to contend with one another as well as with Somerled. Eventually his men must have outnumbered the Vikings but this could probably have happened more quickly if the clans had joined forces in common cause against the enemy early in the campaign. Unfortunately, divisive rivalry was a notable feature of the clans right up to the eighteenth century.

It can only be assumed that, in order to win back all of Argyll, Somerled had to take the whole of the Isle of Mull from the Norse. His early capture of only the north and east of the island, bordering on the Sound, was not enough. Mull was larger than Morvern, and strategically placed for control of the Hebrides. It was also, unfortunately, infested by Norsemen whose principal bases are remembered in their Norse names. The main bases were at Loch na Keal, halfway down the Atlantic west side; Ulva, the island at its mouth; and Fionnphort, opposite Iona. After a considerable struggle Somerled succeeded in driving the Norsemen out of Morvern, Lochaber, Ardgour and north Argyll, then turned his attention to south Argyll and the other Argyll islands.

Having retaken these lands Somerled then had the problem of holding on to them, and it must have been evident to him from the very beginning that castles were essential, especially in order to defend seaways and harbours. It is probable that he copied the basic design of Castle Sween in Knapdale which he would have seen on his frequent journeys up and down the Argyll coast, for all castles built by him are constructed in similar style. This is the oldest stone castle in Scotland, built in the late eleventh century by Suibhne, son of Hugh Anrahan, brother of the king of Ulster and High King of Ireland who had married a princess of Argyll, gaining Knapdale and Cowal as her dowry. Probably he acknowledged the King of Scots as his overlord, for the castle was built in the Norman style – the first in Scotland. Suibhne would have required the tacit approval of the king before being permitted to build such a fortress.

In Somerled's time Suibhne's grandson, Ewan MacSuibhne, held the castle and the land around Loch Sween (or Suibhne).

Somerled began to build a chain of strongholds at strategic places from Skipness in Kintyre to Tioram in Moidart, and probably repaired and strengthened existing ones in order to protect what he now held. The furthest north was Castle Tioram on its island at the head of Loch Moidart.

1138 is the date given for the building of the castle at Loch Finlaggan on Islay – the one most closely associated with Somerled and the later Lords of the Isles, as it became their main residence in the fourteenth and fifteenth centuries. It was their administrative centre and the meeting place for the Councils of the Isles, and was built on two islands just off the northern shore of Loch Finlaggan – Eilean Mòr (Big Island) and Eilean na Comhairle (Island of the Council). The loch lies in an unspectacular, gently curving saucer of moorland, well inland from the sea, its open aspect making it impossible for anyone to approach unseen. The choice of Islay as a main base shows its important position in the centre of the Isles kingdom, and although

Ruins of Finlaggan Castle, Islay. This became the main residence of the Lords of the Isles.

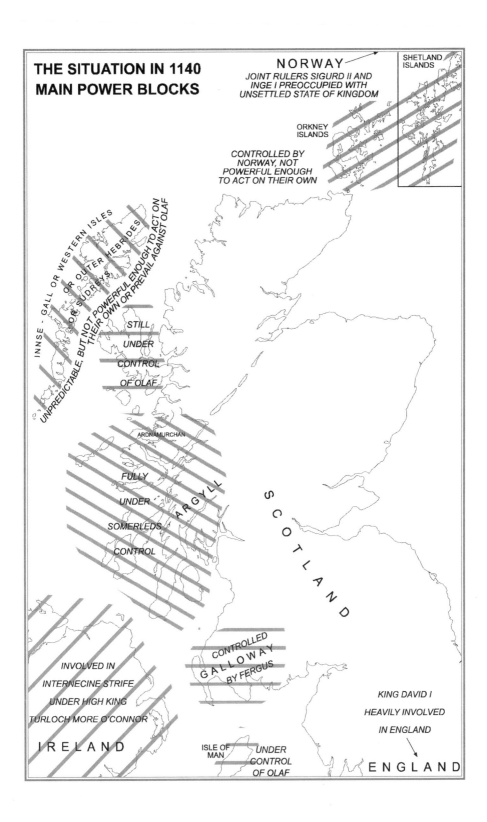

**THE SITUATION IN 1140
MAIN POWER BLOCKS**

NORWAY
*JOINT RULERS SIGURD II AND
INGE I PREOCCUPIED WITH
UNSETTLED STATE OF KINGDOM*

SHETLAND
ISLANDS

ORKNEY
ISLANDS

*CONTROLLED BY
NORWAY, NOT
POWERFUL ENOUGH
TO ACT ON THEIR OWN*

INNSE - GALL OR WESTERN ISLES

OR OUTER HEBRIDES

OR SUDREYS

*UNPREDICTABLE, BUT NOT POWERFUL ENOUGH TO ACT ON
THEIR OWN OR PREVAIL AGAINST OLAF*

*STILL
UNDER
CONTROL
OF OLAF*

ARDNAMURCHAN

*FULLY
UNDER
SOMERLEDS
CONTROL*

ARGYLL

SCOTLAND

*CONTROLLED
GALLOWAY
BY FERGUS*

*INVOLVED IN
INTERNECINE STRIFE
UNDER HIGH KING
TURLOCH MORE O'CONNOR*

IRELAND

ISLE OF
MAN

*UNDER
CONTROL
OF OLAF*

*KING DAVID I
HEAVILY INVOLVED
IN ENGLAND*

ENGLAND

Finlaggan has not yet been completely excavated, it seems never to have been a heavily fortified stronghold. Obviously, by this time Somerled felt safe enough here, in the midst of his far flung territories

Even while driving out the Norse and consolidating his gains in the west it is possible that Somerled became involved in the politics of Scotland through his relationship with the MacHeths, direct challengers to the kings of Scotland. Somerled's sister is said to have married Malcolm, Earl of Ross, and younger brother of Angus, Earl of Moray. The family name of MacHeth originates from their father, Aodh, son-in-law of King Lulach, and descendant of King Malcolm I. 'Son of Aodh', in Gaelic, becomes 'MacAodh', and Gaelic speakers will recognise that in Celtic phonetics this can take the form of 'MacHeth' or 'MacKay' or 'MacGee'. But, although Somerled probably tacitly supported Angus' rebellions in 1124 and 1130, both as a relative, and as a Celtic opponent of the Normanising of Scotland by Scottish kings, there are no sources directly implicating him in the uprisings. Indeed, it seems unlikely that he was able, or willing, to divert his resources from the fraught situation in Argyll and the Isles at this critical time.

In addition, King David I and Somerled seemed to enjoy, if not actually friendly relations, at least considerable respect for one another, so much so that David granted the Firth of Clyde islands of Arran and Bute to Somerled in 1135. He was unlikely to have rewarded a rebellious subject in such a generous fashion.

Possibly David also considered it politic to remain on good terms with this western chief who could deal with the Norse for him, and thus keep Argyll within the kingdom of Scotland without any effort or expense on his part. Also, Arran in particular was within sight, and easy striking distance, of David's lowland Ayrshire and Renfrewshire shores, across the ten to fifteen-mile-wide Firth of Clyde. All the more reason to make Somerled beholden to him by the gift of the islands – a cheap bargain at the price, and an effective plug of a security loophole.

Arran and Bute had been nominally under the control of Walter Fitzallan, the High Steward of Scotland, who seems to have shown no interest in them, as the larger island, Arran, was fairly unproductive, infertile and not of any particular importance to him. To Somerled, however, Arran and Bute in the wrong hands, especially Norse hands, constituted a threat to the security of the whole of southern Argyll, especially Kintyre, which is separated from Argyll by Kilbrannan Sound – a mere three miles at the narrowest part. The Norse undoubtedly had settled there, and the indigenous Celtic population had been demoralised and unable to resist them, having had no aid from the Steward or the king of Scots, until the advent of Somerled's longships.

The situation was thus mutually advantageous to David and to Somerled. On the whole the king seemed to have got the better bargain, for as Somerled's overlord he could call in the Argyll forces for help when he needed them. For example, there were arguments over the English succession on the death of Henry I, and David invaded England to support his niece, the Empress Matilda, in 1135 and 1138. His army was rather a mixed bag and included some of Somerled's men, even although the Norse presence was strong in the Isles at this time. Ailred of Rievaux reports on David's army containing men from the Lothians in the third rank, along with the Islanders and men from the Lorn district of Argyll.

The fact of King David's overlordship of mainland Argyll at this time cannot be contested for he granted to the Church of the Holy Trinity in Dunfermline half the tithes from Argyll and Kintyre which he himself had been accustomed to receiving. He could not have done this without having a royal right to do so.

Somerled's base was now so secure that he could consider casting his net even wider. His neighbour to the south was the Norse king of Man and the Isles, Olaf Godredsson, also known as Olaf the Red. The extent of his kingdom was the archipelago of islands from Man to Lewis with the exception of the Argyll islands, that is, those south of the Ardnamurchan peninsula. The population of these islands was a mixture of Norse, Gall-Gàidheil and Celt. It must have come into Somerled's mind that he should and could attempt to take control not only of his inheritance of Argyll but also of the entire kingdom of Man and the Isles, this being the only effective way of removing the baleful presence of the Norwegians, once and for all. Whether it was his intention, right from the start of his leadership, to establish a wholly Gaelic kingdom in place of the Norse one, is debatable, but possibly the idea took hold as his control over the western seas progressed.

In practice, two kings (Somerled's power was such that he could now be considered a king, or sub-king) with powerful fleets were sharing the same waters – a difficult situation in which to maintain the peace. No doubt skirmishes occurred. However, in accordance with Olaf's stated policy of deliberately cultivating friendship with any potential enemy he made overtures of peace and friendship to Somerled and cemented these by arranging a marriage between his daughter, Ragnhildis, and Somerled. The story goes that Somerled did not take much persuading, having fallen hopelessly in love with the fair lady!

The marriage took place in 1140. The friendly union of the two kingdoms thus increased their fleet capacity enormously and extended their sphere of influence. In addition, Olaf had married as his second wife, Affrica, daughter of Fergus, Lord of Galloway, about 1130. Although Fergus was, at best, a fickle ally, his impressive fleet, added to those of Olaf and Somerled, created a formidable deterrent to any would-be aggressor on the western seaboard – such as King Stephen of England, whose acquisitive Norman lords were always seeking to expand their territories, or the Dublin Norse, also possessors of good fleets, and rank opportunists.

Also, for Somerled, it was a good move to have the unpredictable Fergus on his side, as the latter's Galloway lands ended where Somerled's recent acquisitions Arran and Bute began, thus protecting the south-eastern flanks of Argyll. As for Olaf, an alliance with the powerful Somerled would be an undoubted assurance against any possible treacherous attack by Fergus, whose status as his father-in-law did not automatically guarantee freedom from Galloway attack.

By 1140 then, the kingdoms of Man and Argyll, with their ally, Galloway, looked powerful and impregnable.

CHAPTER FOURTEEN

King of Argyll and
Lord of the Isles

Before considering Somerled's further progress it would be useful to look back to the year 1134 and the latest MacHeth rebellion, this time by Malcolm, Earl of Ross, Somerled's brother-in-law.

As the younger brother of the late Angus, Earl of Moray, killed in the rebellion of 1130, Malcolm now considered the time ripe for another attempt on the Scottish throne – after all, King David was greatly preoccupied in England, laying claim to Northumbria, part of his late wife's estate.

Also, King Henry I was dying and anxious that his brother-in-law, David, should support his daughter and sole legitimate heir, Matilda, against the usurper, Stephen of Blois (Henry's nephew). It looked, therefore, as if David were about to become deeply embroiled in the south for some time – safely out of Malcolm's way.

In addition Malcolm had his brother's death to avenge and, in his estimation anyway, a strong claim to the Scottish throne through the senior Moray line descending from Malcolm I, via King Lulach, and also, possibly as the illegitimate son of Alexander I.

As one of the seven great Celtic Rì he assumed that he could count upon the other six, and on the abbots and bishops of the largely displaced Columban Church, to support his attempt. The Celtic North and the Celtic Church undoubtedly did hate the Margaretsons with their grasping Norman barons, their feudalism and their imposition of the Roman Church, largely instigated by Queen Margaret herself.

But this hoped-for Celtic support was, perhaps, a dangerous assumption on Malcolm's part. King David had been well established as monarch since 1124, and it had been the Celtic Rì themselves who had accepted him as their rightful king.

As Malcolm saw it, although Somerled was not one of the Rì, he was his brother-in-law, and if he, Malcolm, were successful in gaining the throne, Somerled would be well placed to gain a high position in the new king's Court. No doubt Malcolm hoped that this was an attractive enough incentive to bring in Somerled, and if Somerled came in then Olaf and Fergus might come in also all, of course, bringing their fleets with them. These could mount a concerted and mortal attack up the Firth of Clyde into the heartland of south and central Scotland, making, with the men of Moray and the North, a pincer movement around David's forces.

Unfortunately for Malcolm this assumption of support was unfounded for neither Somerled nor the Celtic Rì became involved. Malcolm, inevitably, was defeated by King David and imprisoned in the fortress of Roxburgh.

Apart from his friendship with the king, Somerled may have remained loyal to David because of more pressing local affairs than the grandiose ambitions of Malcolm. The islands were still under continual threat from predators. For example, we hear from *The Book of Islay*, that in 1135 Cadwallader, Prince of Gwynedd, attacked the Western Isles. This was a serious attack, right on his own doorstep, and one which Somerled could not afford to ignore. Diverting men and ships to aid Malcolm was not an option at this time. At any rate there is no reference in the sources to any intervention in Malcolm's rebellion, by Somerled and his allies.

This, no doubt, sent a message of reassurance to David about Somerled's continuing loyalty, and of warning to the Rì that Somerled could not be counted upon to risk his newly recovered kingdom for any political adventurings in mainland Scotland.

Perhaps, too, King David sent a similarly reassuring message back to Somerled by refraining from executing Malcolm, a rebel three times over, as might have been expected, but instead by imposing a mere imprisonment in the king's own presence at Roxburgh. David had stayed his hand most mercifully, and neither the Rì nor Somerled had any excuse to avenge Malcolm who had, for those days, been treated unusually leniently. Careful diplomacy all round. Somerled could concentrate on the consolidation and expansion of his own kingdom.

As has been mentioned in the previous chapter Somerled and Olaf were now sharing the same waters. Somerled controlled the Argyll islands of Islay, Jura, Mull, Gigha, Colonsay, Coll and Tiree while Olaf's kingdom was divided awkwardly into the Isle of Man and the islands north of the Ardnamurchan peninsula, that is Skye and the

Western Isles. It is probable that the two kings co-operated in the task of controlling the entire seaboard, to their mutual advantage. The following report of ruthless reprisals against enemies would seem to confirm this partnership. The story goes that Olaf and Somerled went on an expedition to punish their enemy, MacLier, who owned Strath in the Isle of Skye. After killing him they then prevailed upon a hermit, the strangely named MacPoke, to kill Godfrey Dubh who had previously killed MacPoke's father. Olaf then went on to North Uist where he killed MacNicol. Savage times!

Then, in 1142, trouble broke out in Ireland and soon the Hebrides were in turmoil again. Viking kinglets were for ever squabbling over Irish territories and King Ronald Thorkelssonn of Dublin had been killed by Ottar Ottarssonn, grandson of a previous king of Dublin. Inevitably in 1148, Ottar, King of the Dublin Norse, was killed by the sons of Thorkell.

Because of the intermeshed alliances some factions were for Ottar, and some against, but the danger was that the Nordreys, the Sudreys and Skye could become involved as they were all within the sphere of influence of the Orkney Earls, who were themselves subject to the kings of Norway. Somerled had to be very much on his guard against an escalation of this fracas into a full-scale war.

Probably he had increasingly to shoulder the major part of the burden of policing the Isles as Olaf was now an old man and one who, in any case, had never shown the usual Norse enthusiasm for warfare.

Then a series of significant events occurred which was to alter the power blocks on the map of Scotland yet again.

Firstly, and devastatingly for Somerled, King David died at Carlisle in May 1153, leaving his young, impressionable grandson Malcolm to become king. Somerled's royal ally had gone. The new 12-year-old king was entirely controlled by the Norman barons who had been increasingly grasping control of Scotland during the later years of David's life. David seemed to have lost all spirit for living after the untimely death of his son, Prince Henry, the year previously. There never had been any love lost between the Norman incomers and the Celtic lords of Scotland, so it was unlikely that the young Malcolm IV, so strongly influenced by the Normans, would have enjoyed the same easy relationship with Somerled as his grandfather had done. No doubt the Normans at Court felt that their chance had now come to strike a blow against the Celtic North and these troublesome western chiefs, Somerled, Olaf and Fergus.

Meanwhile, Malcolm MacHeth, still languishing in prison after his last abortive attempt to take the throne, was in great danger of his life now that his protector had died. Certainly the only reason why the Normans might keep him alive would be to pose the threat of his instant execution should Somerled and the Celts attempt another rising. Malcolm was, of course, one of the Celtic Rì, the seven great earls of Scotland, who normally elect a Scottish king, and was eligible to be elected king himself, but this no longer of any relevance in the opinion of the Normans.

King David had continued the now established system of primogeniture, according to the feudal fashion, by declaring his son, Henry, the next king of Scotland, then, on the latter's death, his first-born grandson, Malcolm. The Celtic system of the Tanist had gone for good, but the Rì had yet to accept it. It was the case that all Celtic Scotland was ready to rise in rebellion and Somerled with them, regardless of the threat to Malcolm MacHeth's life. Somerled had paid homage to King David, but had noticeably not done so to King Malcolm IV. And so, in 1153, *The Chronicle of Holyrood* reports that Somerled and his MacHeth nephews gathered together a large army of supporters and rampaged throughout Scotland, defying King Malcolm's power.

Olaf of Man would have been a useful ally in this troubled situation, especially as he owed allegiance only to the king of Norway and not to the Scots king, but Olaf was now a tired old man. And the next blow was to fall here, in 1153.

King Olaf's fiercely Norse son, Godred or Godfrey the Black, was safely out of the Manx kingdom, at the court of King Inge of Norway, and the way was now clear for Olaf's three nephews, sons of his brother Harald of Dublin, to come over to visit their elderly uncle. Taking advantage of his weakness they made aggressive demands that he hand over to them half his kingdom. Olaf tried his usual policy of appeasement – upon which he had built and held his kingdom for 50 years – and was murdered for his pains. The aggressors then rampaged throughout Man, totally out of control. The danger to Somerled was that they might look northwards towards his kingdom with greedy eyes. As Olaf had grown older his kingdom had become extremely vulnerable to potential attack by predatory Norse, Norman-Scots or English. The Manx kingdom in the wrong hands would be a constant threat to Argyll's security.

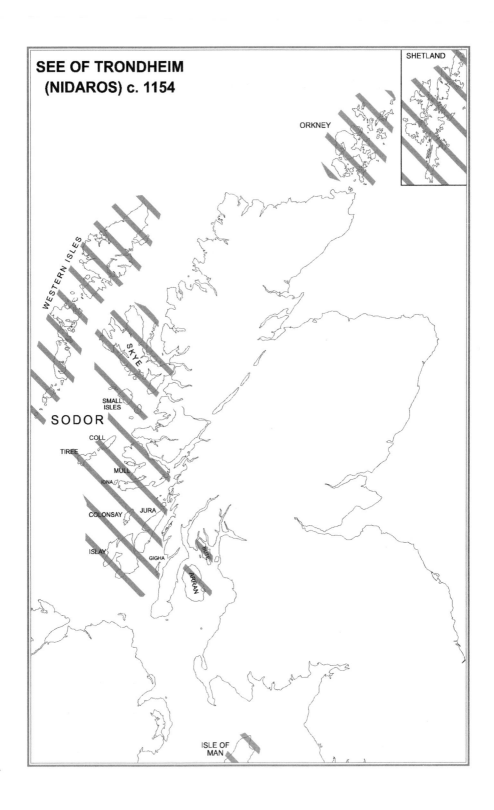

SEE OF TRONDHEIM
(NIDAROS) c. 1154

SHETLAND

ORKNEY

WESTERN ISLES

SKYE

SMALL
ISLES

SODOR

COLL

TIREE

MULL

IONA

COLONSAY   JURA

ISLAY   GIGHA

BUTE

ARRAN

ISLE OF
MAN

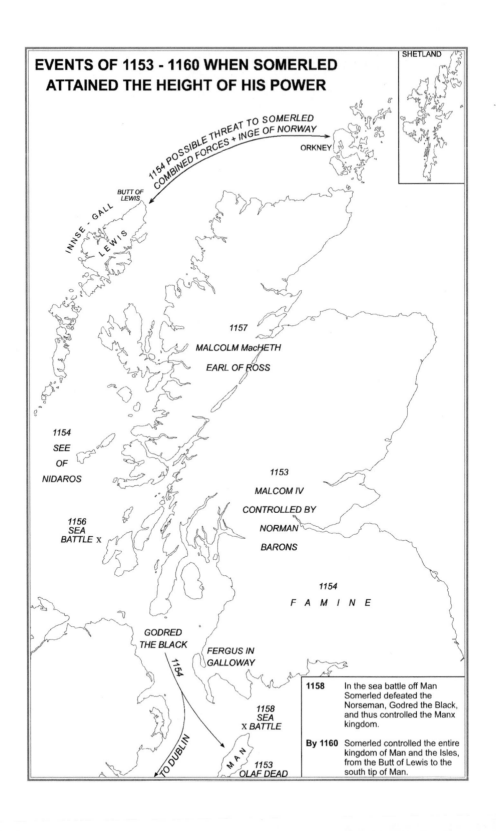

EVENTS OF 1153 - 1160 WHEN SOMERLED ATTAINED THE HEIGHT OF HIS POWER

SHETLAND

1154 POSSIBLE THREAT TO SOMERLED
COMBINED FORCES + INGE OF NORWAY

ORKNEY

BUTT OF
LEWIS

INNSE - GALL

LEWIS

1157

MALCOLM MacHETH

EARL OF ROSS

1154
SEE
OF
NIDAROS

1153

MALCOM IV

CONTROLLED BY

NORMAN

BARONS

1156
SEA
BATTLE x

1154

F A M I N E

GODRED
THE BLACK

FERGUS IN
GALLOWAY

1154

TO DUBLIN

M A N

1158
SEA
X BATTLE

1153
OLAF DEAD

1158	In the sea battle off Man Somerled defeated the Norseman, Godred the Black, and thus controlled the Manx kingdom.
By 1160	Somerled controlled the entire kingdom of Man and the Isles, from the Butt of Lewis to the south tip of Man.

With King David gone and the Normans out to grab as much land, power and high office as they could, Somerled could not hope for any help against Man from the royal forces, especially as he had so recently taken part in another MacHeth rising against the king. He was now isolated in his western kingdom. There was no Olaf to act as ally against King Malcolm and his Normans; the Dublin Norse usurpers in Man might attack him from the south and even if they could be neutralised this very fact might cause a power vacuum in the Hebrides which several opportunists might attempt to fill. It wasn't really to be supposed that Olaf's nephews could hold the kingdom for any length of time. They were no strategists and their judgment was at fault. After all, they had rashly decided to attack Fergus' Galloway, been routed, and retreated hurriedly and in disorder to Man.

A bigger threat was the possible interest of the earls of Orkney with their large fleets, including those of the Norse of Innse-Gall. They were very familiar with these waters through years of trading with the Norse-Irish. They could fill any power vacuum very efficiently indeed.

Worst of all, King Inge of Norway, with all the might of his great fleet, might turn his attention to the Manx kingdom. This would mean not just an attack on Man, but war for Argyll and its Isles.

Fergus of Galloway, the third member of the earlier western alliance, who might have been expected to offer aid to Somerled, showed no eagerness whatever to avenge the death of his son-in-law Olaf. As a powerful Celtic lord, situated geographically close to lowland Scotland, his proximity was dangerous to King Malcolm whose Norman barons were about to stretch out their mailed fists to deal with him, thereby striking a blow at Celtic Scotland.

And now the third significant event occurred which affected the balance of power on the western seaboard. Olaf's son, Godred the Black, came back from Norway to regain his rightful kingdom, with the support, and probably the ships, of Orkney and Norway. He invaded Man, seized the three sons of Harald and killed them in vengeance for his father's death. Then the Dublin Norse appointed him as their king.

This must have appeared initially to be the answer to Somerled's prayer. A strong Manx king along with his allies could keep the previously volatile local situation in hand. King Muirchertach of Ireland tried to wrest back Dublin out of Godred's hands but was roundly defeated. Godred appeared to be firmly in control of his father's kingdom.

Unfortunately Godred proved to be very different kind of king from his father and, as the *Chronicle of Man* described it, as soon as he had established total control over Man he started to harass the local chiefs, going so far as to remove all powers from them, and even throwing them off their lands.

This, in itself, was not enough to make Somerled move against Godred, but in 1154 other news of an ecclesiastical nature hinted at probable collusion between Godred and King Inge of Norway. Pope Anastasius IV had appointed the Bishop of the Sudreys as Suffragan to the new Metropolitan See of Nidaros in Norway which included in its scope Orkney, Shetland and the Hebrides. Norway would thus obtain an ecclesiastical foothold in these areas, no doubt as the first step towards political interference there too. It looked very much as if Godred had agreed to include the Manx kingdom in this arrangement in order to get Norwegian support for his attempt to regain his patrimony, and then probably to push back Somerled from all of the islands.

The *Chronicle of Man* takes up the story again concerning events which were to bring Somerled and Godred into open conflict. It tells how Thorfinn Ottarsson, a powerful Manx chief, was sent to ask Somerled to allow his son, Dugall, to be appointed king of Man and the Isles. After due consideration Somerled was pleased to allow Dugall to be presented as king to the islanders, who duly accepted him though hostages were taken to ensure their continued compliance!

Acceptance, however, was not unanimous, and one of the chiefs, named Paul Balkanson, slipped away by night in his longship and went to Godred with the news of all that had occurred. Godred, in alarm, hurriedly got ready a fleet and sailed north against the forces of Somerled.

It was high time for Somerled to do something about Godred. He, in his turn, collected a large fleet of eighty longships and sailed out to confront his enemy.

The story that follows incites our admiration for the impressive seamanship of both kings, and the seaworthiness of their ships. The battle took place at night, in the dead of winter, in the open ocean somewhere off the coasts of Islay, on the 5–6 January 1156. How they managed to manoeuvre under oars (no sails were used during battle), in darkness, in wild winter seas, without most of their ships colliding or foundering, was a miracle. It must have been a titanic struggle and

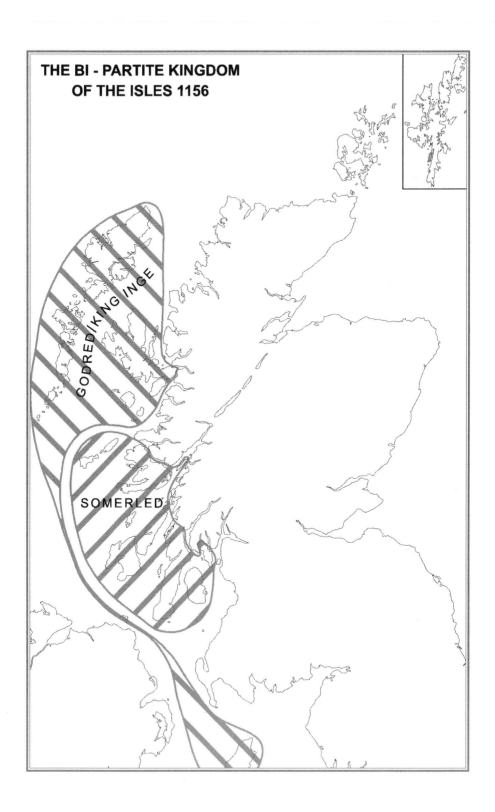

THE BI - PARTITE KINGDOM
OF THE ISLES 1156

GODRED|KING INGE

SOMERLED

the *Chronicle of Man* describes the terrible slaughter which ensued. By dawn both sides were exhausted, neither having won, so they agreed to make peace and divided up the sea kingdom between them, in a rather awkward division.

Godred retained Man and the islands to the north of the Ardnamurchan peninsula, while Somerled kept all the islands to the south including Kintyre, which was still classed as an island. King Inge of Norway must have accepted this arrangement, at least for the time being, for there was no Norwegian counter-attack in support of his protégé, Godred.

There now followed a series of distractions for Somerled. Events in Scotland had temporarily attracted the attention of the Scottish court away from the west to the mainland itself. The *Chronicle of Holyrood* tells us that there was a terrible famine in the land, as a result of a cattle epidemic. In addition to this catastrophe, King Stephen of England died in November, and Henry, Duke of Normandy, became king. Then Duncan, Earl of Fife, died.

These events turned Scotland in on itself. The plague affected not only the meat supplies, but also the draught animals for ploughing, which in turn led to a decimated harvest.

The accession of Henry II in England brought anxiety to the Scottish Normans as they feared that the ambitious and hot-tempered Henry would cast covetous eyes on their recently acquired power, wealth and land.

The death of the Earl of Fife, one of the influential Celtic Rì and thereby the loss of his considerable forces, was bound to have weakened the effect of the new rising by Donald MacHeth, son of the imprisoned Malcolm, in 1153. Somerled, however, threw in the power of his forces, not only in support of the MacHeths, but also to protest about court intrigues which attempted to undermine his own position as a powerful western leader. The uprising lasted for three years during which Galloway was also implicated, but the Normans prevailed and the *Chronicle of Melrose* reports that Donald MacHeth was captured at Whithorn, and thrown into prison at Roxburgh alongside his father.

The MacHeths truly seemed to lead charmed lives, for yet again the Scots king refrained from executing them. *The Clan Donald* offers the explanation that Malcolm IV was seriously intimidated by Somerled's aggression and considering commonsense to be the better part of valour, decided to offer terms of peace, which were indeed accepted by Somerled. So a treaty was drawn up in 1157 by which Donald MacHeth was freed, and Malcolm MacHeth given the valuable earldom of Ross.

The MacHeth problem appeared, finally, to have been solved, and Somerled needed no longer to involve himself with the now dead concept of an alternative succession to the Scottish throne – at least for the present.

The year 1158, unfortunately, saw Somerled's attention brought sharply back to events in the west. The situation in Man was simmering again. It was obvious that Godred would not accept the imposition of Somerled's son, Dugall, as king of Man, without a fight. Somerled must have recognised that Godred would have to be dealt with once and for all, and that battle was inevitable. The *Chronicle of Man* tells how, in 1158, Somerled sailed with 53 ships and engaged Godred's fleet off the coast of Man. Not only did Somerled finally rout Godred at sea, but he then brought his forces ashore and, by capturing or destroying all who opposed him, brought the entire island into submission before returning in triumph to his own waters. Godred managed to escape and fled back to Norway, hoping to get help against the all-powerful Somerled.

But Godred the Black never challenged Somerled again, and left him in possession of the Manx kingdom for the rest of his life. Again, the Norwegian king did not intervene on Godred's behalf, so we must assume his tacit acceptance of the situation.

Somerled was now, truly, King of Argyll and Lord of the Isles.

Final Campaign

By 1160 Somerled was at the height of his power. His kingdom extended from the Butt of Lewis to the most southerly point of Man. Malcolm, King of Scots, was looking favourably upon him, for he gave a charter on 25 December 1160 at Perth, dating it on the Christmas Day after the peace treaty between himself and Somerled.

Perth, in 1160, was also the scene of an attack by the five remaining Rì against Malcolm IV, led by Feradach of Strathearn. They were angered by Malcolm's prolonged absence from Scotland with the army of King Henry II at Toulouse. Malcolm appeared to be Henry's man, rather than Scotland's king and so they besieged Perth and unsuccessfully attempted to capture the king. Somerled did not take part in this rising. The peace between him and the king held.

The king of Scots and his Norman barons were now free of two of their most pressing problems: the MacHeths, who were now firmly under royal control, and the unpredictable Godred of Man, who had been most effectively dealt with by Somerled. It was time to turn their attention to that most potent threat in the south-west, Fergus of Galloway. The *Chronicle of Holyrood* describes how, in 1160, King Malcolm's army invaded Galloway on three occasions and defeated Fergus' men, after which he was able to impose his own terms of peace. Fergus seems to have finally lost heart in the face of the superior weight of royal arms and retreated into the religious life, by becoming a canon in the church of Holyrood in Edinburgh. Later, as proof of his devotion he gave the village of Dunrod to the church.

The Wolf of Galloway seems to have been well and truly tamed. This story had an unexpectedly swift ending, for the *Chronicle of Holyrood* goes on to say that Fergus, Prince of Galloway, died in May 1161.

And now it appeared that there were two kings in Scotland. Somerled was paramount in the west for his potential opponents, the kings of Ireland and Norway, were otherwise engaged.

Muirchertach Uí-Lochlann was the recently acknowledged High King of Ireland, and currently at war with his vassal kings. He had neither the time nor the inclination to challenge Somerled's invincible hold on the Western Isles.

Far from challenging Somerled's position, King Inge of Norway seems to have bowed to the inevitable, for *The Book of Islay* tells us that in 1160 Somerled obtained the title, from Inge, of king of the Sudreys. He was not recognised as ruler of all the Norse possessions in Scotland for Godred the Black, according to the *Icelandic Annals*, became king of the Hebrides in the same year. The probable explanation of Inge's acceptance of both Somerled and Godred is that he had formally approved the original agreement between the two men over the division of the islands in 1156. Somerled must have accepted the Norwegian king as his suzerain, in return for the Sudreys, but did not feel threatened by that fact.

Although there is no formal evidence of exactly how Somerled ruled his territories at this time, there is a mention of some of his activities in the list of Cistercian Foundations of 1160, in connection with the foundation of Saddell Abbey in Kintyre, which he or his son, Reginald, promoted. Also, it appears that Somerled was anxious to bring back the glory to Iona, for the *Annals of Ulster* describe a meeting in Ireland in 1164 between dignitaries of the community of Iona and the Irish ecclesiastic, Flaithbertach u-Brolchain, to offer him the successorship of Iona, in council with Somerled and the men of Argyll and the Hebrides. But King Muirchertach of Ireland did intervene in Somerled's affairs in this instance, and would not permit it.

Between the years 1160 and 1163 King Malcolm IV had concerned himself more with foreign affairs than with events at home. In order to increase his prestige he had arranged the marriage, in 1162, of his sister, Ada, with the Count Florence of Holland, rather surprisingly offering, as her dowry, the earldom of Ross, already granted to Malcolm MacHeth in 1157. But, in fact, Malcolm retained the earldom until his death.

Then, in 1163, King Malcolm's attention was turned to domestic matters. King Henry II had come home to England from abroad, and was met by Malcolm who suddenly became seriously ill. Although he made a good recovery, perhaps his will had been weakened by his illness for he accepted firm peace terms with Henry, having been forced to hand over Northumbria and Cumbria in exchange for the earldom of Huntingdon. Worse still, according to the *Chronicle of Holyrood*, he allowed his brother David, along with some other young noblemen, to be taken as hostages to the English court.

Although the king of Scots had been humiliated in this way by the king of England, at least he was free, for some time, from further English aggression, and was able to turn his full attention to the threat with which Somerled faced him in 1164.

Why Somerled decided to mount his fatal expedition against the king has never been documented and theories abound.

Perhaps by this time he was appalled by the weakness of a king of Scots who had so humbled himself and Scotland, by accepting his knighthood from the king of England, and who had done homage for his English lands, like any ordinary English lord.

Possibly, also, Somerled apprehensively anticipated the imminent annexation of Scotland by Henry – who was in possession of a powerful fleet, unlike his predecessor, King Stephen – and decided on a pre-emptive strike.

After all, Scotland, at this time, was by no means a united country with the consciousness of a single national identity. Somerled may have felt it necessary to protest against what he perceived to be the submersion of Scotland under an ever-increasing sea of Normans holding high offices of state and already in possession of vast tracts of Scottish territory, and who no doubt hoped to crush him in order to get his kingdom for division among themselves.

It is possible that Somerled was not aiming at the throne of Scotland but at the recognition of Argyll as an independent kingdom which would be inherited in the normal fashion by his sons and their descendants, especially as Malcolm was apparently an ineffectual king who had been faced with rebellions throughout the length of his reign. Malcolm would have found it impossible to hold on to his throne if all the various factions had got together and acted in concert against him.

There is also the fact that Malcolm and Somerled fundamentally distrusted one another, standing, as they did, for radically different systems of government – Somerled for the Celtic, and Malcolm for the Feudal.

In addition, Somerled's confidence in Malcolm's integrity must have been undermined by the ease with which Malcolm was prepared to hand over Malcolm MacHeth's earldom of Ross as his sister's dowry in 1162. Was such a weak and vacillating man worthy of the throne of Scotland, and of Somerled's support? Opinions on this subject are many and varied. The historian, George Buchanan, in his *History of Scotland*, referred to Somerled as the Thane of Argyll who desired only to become sovereign of Scotland, but his account of Somerled's life shows little factual evidence to support this comment.

The *Chronicle of Man* agreed with Buchanan that Somerled gathered together a fleet of ships in which he sailed to the Renfrewshire shores, with the sole purpose of conquering Scotland.

Donald Gregory, in his *History of the Western Highlands and Islands of Scotland*, also puts down Somerled's motives to personal ambition, as did WF Skene in his Introduction to the *Book of the Dean of Lismore*.

The contemporary writer, Roger Hoveden, in his *Chronica*, gave an opinion fairly typical of the times, that the expedition was merely an act of rebellion common enough in the twelfth century when he wrote, of the year 1164 that Somerled, 'under-king' of Argyll, rebelled against King Malcolm, his lawful king.

The Clan Donald authors, as might be expected, took a more charitable view and suggested that for Somerled to have attacked Scotland in order to obtain the throne would have been right out of character, and inconsistent with his previous good judgment even during the most troublesome parts of his life. They held Malcolm himself responsible for the attack by saying that he wanted to extend his royal authority over all Scotland, including the outland territories of what is now Mid-Argyll, Kintyre and Lorn.

Nowadays we may find it unsurprising that the king of Scots should want to control the entire land mass of Scotland, but in the twelfth century not everyone saw it that way.

For example, Hugh MacDonald's *History of the Macdonalds* puts forward Somerled's supposed reply, that his mainland territories had been in the family since time immemorial, but had been stolen from his forebears by MacBeth, and that the islands had been granted to the family by King Eugenius I. Somerled is also supposed to have complained that none of the kings of Scotland had ever helped the family to protect these lands against Norse incursions, and that therefore the aforesaid lands were his, and his alone. He did, however, accede that he would give his assistance to the king in connection with any other matters, and would prove to be as loyal as anyone else, but that as long as he lived he refused utterly to give up any of his territories or rights, to any man. He said that he would either lose it all, or keep it all.

The Clan Donald authors comment that Somerled's action was part of a long-expected movement by the Celtic peoples against the apparent policy of the Crown to crush the independent lords of Scotland one by one, giving, as example, Malcolm's invasion of Galloway and Moray in 1160 after which he brought in southerners in large numbers and imposed them on the lands of the displaced native folk – a forerunner of the later Clearances. They go on to say that there was no doubt in the minds of the Celtic chiefs about what Malcolm was up to in 1160, and that no doubt Somerled, by invading in 1164, was merely trying to take the heat off them, by diverting the king's forces.

Whatever his motive there is no doubt that Somerled felt confident enough to challenge the king. He had the ships, the men, the fighting experience and he no doubt felt that he also had the moral backing of Gaelic Scotland, with every expectation that the Rì would rise to support him. It was time to take the most momentous step of his hitherto brilliantly successful career.

The *Annals of Ulster* describes the large force which embarked with Somerled in 1164 as being men from Argyll, Kintyre, the Hebrides, and even Norsemen from Dublin. The fleet was said to have consisted of 164 ships, which sailed up the Clyde to near Renfrew, where the landing was made. Tradition puts the actual battle at the farmstead of Bargarran, near the site of the present Glasgow Airport.

No reliable account exists of the battle which followed and various accounts are given some of which assert that Somerled was killed on the battlefield with his son, Gillecolum, and others that he was killed by treachery. Hugh MacDonald declares that Somerled's sister's son, Maurice MacNeill, a scoundrel, was bribed to kill his uncle by the cowardly Normans who were afraid of being defeated in pitched battle by the ferocious Highlanders. This seems rather unlikely, and was probably a face-saving way of explaining the disastrous defeat which would be more acceptable to the Clan.

The only certainty is that the Rì did not join Somerled, or come to his assistance and that Somerled was undoubtedly killed. He was, after all, a man of about 64 at this time. The *Carmen de Morte Sumerlidi* gives a lengthy and heavily biased description of the defeat of the Celtic host:

And in the first clef of battle the baleful leader fell. Wounded by a [thrown] spear, slain by the sword, Somerled died.

And the raging waves swallowed his son, and the wounded of many thousand fugitives; because when this fierce leader was struck down, the wicked took to flight and very many were slaughtered, both on sea and on land – Thus the enemies' ranks were deluded and repelled; and the whole kingdom with loud voices praised [Saint Kentigern].

After Somerled's death the Highland host vanished away like melting snow, back to where the longships awaited them, and sadly sailed out to the west. The survivors reached home safely, bringing the body of Somerled with them. He is thought to have been buried in the precinct of his own Saddell Abbey in Kintyre but this has never been confirmed. Indeed Hugh MacDonald disputes this, saying that Somerled was buried on Iona, according to the reports of twenty different people on that island.

The disaster at Bargarran was so catastrophic to the Highland cause that there were no further serious challenges to the kings of Scotland by the Gaels for 247 years until the Battle of Harlaw in 1411, but neither did the Crown annexe Somerled's kingdom nor divide it up among the Normans as Somerled had feared. Instead his sons Dugall, Reginald and Angus were left in undisturbed possession of their father's extensive kingdom, which was to go down in history as the renowned Lordship of the Isles.

PART THREE

The Ships

GLOSSARY OF NAUTICAL TERMS

aft:	back or hind end of a ship
beam:	right and left sides of a ship
bow:	front end of a ship where it begins to arch inwards
brace:	a rope attached to the yard, for trimming sails
bulkhead:	upright partition dividing ship's hull into compartments
caulk:	to stop up the seams of a ship with wool, animal hair or oakum dipped in resin, oil or tar
cleat:	wedge-shaped piece of wood projecting from a spar to prevent a rope from slipping
crone:	heavy block of wood resting on the keel and used to support the base of the mast when upright
draught:	depth of water a ship draws or requires to float her
fore:	front part of a ship
garboard strake:	first plank next to keel
gunwale/gunnel:	upper edge of a ship's side
hull:	body framework of a ship
keel:	lowest longitudinal timber of a ship on which the framework of the whole is built up
kerling:	as for crone
lateen:	yard slung slantwise across a mast
port:	left-hand side of a ship when facing forward
portage:	the hauling of a ship overland by means of wooden rollers
prow:	fore part immediately about the stem of a ship
ribs:	ship's curved timbers to which planks are nailed
sheer:	upward slope of a ship's lines towards bow and stern
sheet:	rope attached to the lower corner of a sail for regulating its tension
starboard:	right-hand side of a ship when facing forward
stay:	rope supporting a mast or spar
stem:	carved timber to which a ship's sides are joined at the front end
stern:	hind part of a ship
strake:	continuous line of planking from the stem to the stern of a ship
thwart:	plank or oarsman's bench, placed across a ship
tree nail:	pin of hard wood for securing planks
withy:	tough, flexible, thin branch especially of willow or osier
yard:	cylindrical spar, tapering to each end, and slung horizontally or slantwise across the mast to support a sail

CHAPTER SIXTEEN

Evolution of the Viking Longship

Methinks you know the King?
Dwells at 'Kvinne'
Head of the Norsemen
Master of deep keels
and scarlet shields
tarred oars
and spray-drenched boards

HORNKLOVE: THE SONG OF HARALD

Without the ships the Lordship could not, and would not, have happened. Somerled fought the Vikings, fire with fire, using their very own most effective and formidable weapon – the longship, which he made his own. The above verse of poetry reflects the ship-delight of Norwegians of King Harald Fairhair's time. Their feelings of pride were understandable, for, according to Professor AW Brøgger, Professor of Archaeology, University of Oslo, in *The Viking Ships, Their Ancestry and Evolution*:

> It is the judgement of all experts, foreign as well as native [Norwegian] that better sea-going boats for coast and ocean were never built.

The sea was in the blood of the Norse, and so were the ships, throughout centuries of evolution from the earliest known skin boats, to the longships at the zenith of Norwegian sea power around the mid-thirteenth century. The term 'longship' should be regarded as a collective term covering every type of warship.

In the year 1075 the *Chronicle of Man* tells us of the subjugation of

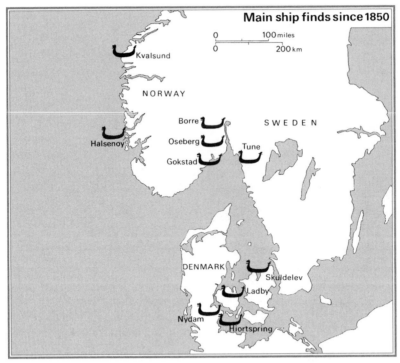

Man, Dublin and Galloway by the Norseman, Godred Crovan, after which he imposed measures to preserve the superiority of his own fine vessels. He warned the Galloway men, with direst threats, that no one should dare presume to build a ship using more than three iron bolts or nails.

Somerled must have realised the importance of getting hold of some of these sleek, manoeuvrable warships if he were to stand any chance of beating his enemies at their own game.

No doubt he acquired some originally by piracy, or as spoils of battle, then finally by having them built by his own shipwrights to the Norse pattern – one which has proved so successful that it has altered very little, in Norway and in Scotland, to this very day. Working wooden fishing boats are currently being built in a boatyard in Stornoway, Isle of Lewis, to a recognisably Norse design.

Ships were of prime importance, not only to Somerled, but to his descendants, and this is recognised in the use of the galley (which evolved out of the longship), in the Clan Donald coat of arms. The ship in the arms of MacDonald of Sleat is a representation of the one in which the three Princes Colla sailed from Ireland to Scotland. Very early seals of the Lords of the Isles depict the ship with rowers in it.

The evolution of the Viking ship is in three stages: the skin boat, the plank boat (clinker built) and the sea-going ship with mast and sail.

The earliest known ancestor of the Viking longship was not the log boat, as might have been expected, but the Stone Age skin boat dating from the ancient sea-hunting culture of north Norway. These boats brought about the settlement of all the westernmost and northernmost islands of Norway where sea fishing was the prime means of survival.

Hooks, harpoons, spears as well as boat remains have been found in these areas. The skin boats, built on ribs, had to be strong and seaworthy enough to cope with such infamous sea areas as the sea of Røst, and the Moskenstrøn, or Maelstrom. A heavy log boat would never have survived in these turbulent seas, even with outriggers for stability, having too much rigidity of structure to avoid swamping. Log boat remains have been found in, or beside, inland lakes and rivers where they were much more suitable. Rock carvings from north Norway show many types of skin boat fishing vessels.

The common feature of them all, which just could not occur in a log boat, is the curving upwards of the prow, and sometimes also the

Coat of Arms of MacDonald of Sleat. This galley represents the ship in which the three Princes Colla sailed over from Ireland to Scotland

Early Scandinavian skin boats

stern, a sophisticated feature which one would hardly expect to find in such early vessels. The transition from the keel to the elevated stem and stern is very sudden and makes the hull look rather rectangular, eg numbers 14 and 33, not possible in either a log or a plank boat. Some also show the presence of bulkheads, which wouldn't be seen in a log boat, eg numbers 3,5,6, 18 and 30, the latter showing a man sitting between the bulkheads. The materials for building such boats were readily available, and reflect the sea-hunting culture – bone and wood

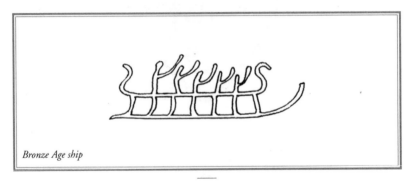

Bronze Age ship

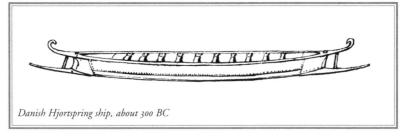

Danish Hjortspring ship, about 300 BC

for the ribs, with seal or other skin stretched tightly over them, making a light yet pliant boat whose flexibility was an advantage in the rough, northern seas.

Ships of the Bronze Age, from about 1500 BC to early Iron Age can be seen in rock carvings at Bardal, Trondelag and Skjeling, Østfold. They also are made of animal skins stretched over ribs, and now show the bottom rib projecting forward and upward, like a beak, to protect the skins when beaching the ship. The vertical strokes represent the crew.

Rock carvings at Brandskog, Uppland, Sweden show an early Iron Age ship where animal heads are now seen on prow and stern – a forerunner of the exquisite carvings to be seen on important Viking longships. The crew stand up to paddle the ship, which could not therefore be an ocean-going vessel.

The second big step forward in evolution was the use of wood in Iron Age shipbuilding, probably as hunters turned their attention to the extensive coastal forests of Norway. Drawings show parallel keel and gunwale, ending fore and aft in upward curving 'beaks'. The hull is built of whole planks, or strakes, of wood, sewn together with spruce roots, or withy, caulked with animal hair and resin or seal oil, and tied to ribs made of pliant hazel branches. The bottom is made of one broad plank and over that two broad but thin planks on either side, the uppermost edge of which is the gunwale. This has been carved to be thicker and stronger in order to withstand hard wear, and to hold the upper hull together. This is clearly seen in the Danish Hjortspring ship of about 300 BC. Note the extension of keel-plank and gunwale into characteristic 'beaks', the ribs reinforced with cross-pieces and props under the thwarts. There were steering oars at each end and room for twenty paddlers. This ship is light, strong and manoeuvrable, and able to take a large crew.

The Halsenoy ship, of about 200 AD shows an important step forward in that paddles now give way to oars.

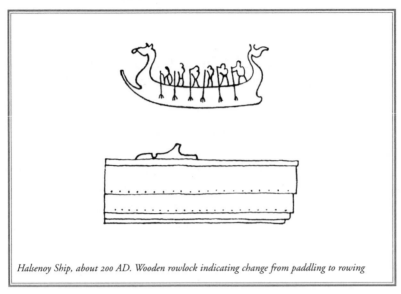

Halsenoy Ship, about 200 AD. Wooden rowlock indicating change from paddling to rowing

This was followed by the Nydam ship, of about 350 AD (dated by Hakon Shetelig, Professor of Archaeology, University of Bergen), constructed rather like the Halsenoy ship, and now with overlapping, (clinker) planking, and this time fastened together with iron nails. The clinker vessel was to keep on improving until it reached the perfection of the Gokstad ship.

The ship now began to look like our expectation of a Viking ship, with high stem and stern, but was fundamentally weak because it still had only a heavy keel-plank and no proper keel. Thus the ship was too narrow and weak to resist sea pressure, and could not possibly support a mast.

The third stage in ship evolution took place with the ship from Kvalsund in Heroy, Sunnmore, dated 600 AD and was a significant technical advance towards the classic Viking longship. The Kvalsund ship had a true external keel, all in one piece, and strong enough to protect the hull against the pressure of the sea. Consequently it could

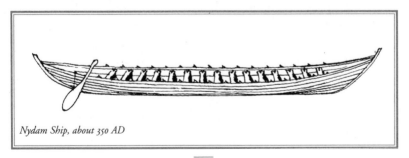

Nydam Ship, about 350 AD

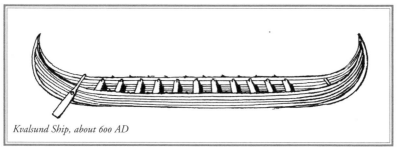

Kvalsund Ship, about 600 AD

be made wider, giving the ship more stability and carrying power. It was about 18 metres long, with a beam of about three metres – still very narrow – and drawing only about 80 centimetres. Instead of only two broad planks per side, the Kvalsund ship had many narrow strakes on each side, tied or nailed together, to give maximum flexing in a big sea.

Of equal importance was the development of the rudder, which was now attached very firmly to the ship's aft, starboard gunwale, with a tiller for ease of steering, replacing the earlier loose steering oars. These two major developments introduced the possibility of having a mast and sails for use in all weathers.

The way was now clear for future North Sea and Atlantic voyages, in the seventh and eighth centuries, at first to the Northern and Western Isles and mainland Scotland, then on to Iceland, Greenland and America, with the subsequent impact we have seen on the populations of these areas, particularly Scotland, and thereby on the life and work of Somerled MacGillebride.

What was now needed, in ship design, was an increase in the strength and stability of the keel, so that a proper mast, capable of carrying a good spread of sail, could be safely raised. Design evolution, during the years between 600 and 900 AD resulted in the famous Gokstad ship which well answered this need.

> Shipbuilding in the Viking Era was the final stage of a long development, the result of seamanship and technical skill which had gradually achieved that classic standard of which the Gokstad ship is an example.
>
> Brøgger & Shetelig, *The Viking Ships, Their Ancestry and Evolution*, 1951

This vessel was the precursor of the Viking longship.

CHAPTER SEVENTEEN

The Gokstad Ship

Brøgger and Shetelig are full of admiration for these early ship designers and builders, particularly when they consider that there were no drawn plans, each man working purely by eye judgment, to a well-established tradition:

> Our first impression of the Gokstad ship is that of a complete harmony of line and form. It is a real work of art, with the full curve of the sides that naturally and organically flows fore and aft into the high, pointed stem and stern. Between them the straight line of the keel runs like the nerve of the structure, coming up fore and aft in a bold thrust to cleave the water and fling it aside. The ship inspires the same delight as a shapely living creature, a paragon of its kind, a system of many parts welded into a perfect unity.

A truly emotional response if ever there was one. But the Gokstad ship was more than an ocean poem. She was a practical, working vessel of the highest efficiency.

By this time the problem of the keel had been overcome and the 'bearing' parts of the ship, ie keel, stem and stern, strakes, ribs with crossbeams and knees were all of oak, the hardest wood available. The keel was one piece and had a T-shaped section notched to give a watertight join with the bottom strakes. Also, its profile showed that it was deeper amidships where the greatest weight would be (mast, kerling and mast-partner), with tapered ends for easy progress through the water. This gave the greatest strength for the least weight. The Norwegian archaeologists also add:

> The keel forms a very flat and even arch from fore to aft so that the ship draws 30cm more amidships than at the ends. This is also a masterly feature, as it makes it easier to turn the

ship about, causing it to lie high on the water, and increases its capacity, as the greatest draught is where the hull is broadest.

This strong keel reinforced the entire length of the ship, enabling it to withstand the pressure of heavy ocean swell. Now, for the first time, the ship was strong enough to sail into the wind, and to stand the hull strain of a beaching.

The stem and stern were each in a single piece, rising in a curve from the keel. The hull was composed of 16 thin strakes per side, joined to each other by iron clench nails or rivets, and overlapping in the characteristic clinker style. During the planking procedure the ship was caulked at the lower edge of each strake with twisted cords of wool or animal hair dipped in tar before being laid in. This made for a very watertight ship. The first nine strakes from the keel were all equally thin (2.6cm), and tied, not nailed, on to the ribs with spruce roots. Each plank was formed by shaving down a board to the required thickness, leaving a protruding cleat in the middle. This was wasteful of materials but meant that cleat and strake were formed in one piece, and thus very strong and stable. Holes were bored through each cleat and its corresponding rib so that spruce roots could be threaded through both, and the whole lashed firmly together. This allowed a certain amount of movement in the hull, so that it did not fight against the sea, but yielded pliantly to the pressure of the waves.

This seemingly tedious procedure was an essential of Viking ship construction and was probably used because it suited the thin, bendable planking. Iron rivets would have required heavier strakes, whereas lighter planking meant a more easily handled ship under oars or sail, or when under portage. This is a way of transporting a ship, by beaching her on to rollers, usually smoothed logs, and pulling her along over the ground. A good example of this method of moving a ship overland is well documented in Magnus Bareleg's Saga when the king had his ship rolled over the isthmus between West and East Loch Tarbert, Kintyre, in 1098.

The tenth strake from the keel, at the waterline, was subject to more stress where it turned from the almost flat underwater section, to the upright sides of the ship. It was 4.4cm thick. In addition this plank had to take the weight of the tops of the ribs and the crossbeams which were added later. Only when the tenth strake was put in were the 19 oak ribs laid on, but not attached to keel or garboard strake. This was commonplace in the Viking Era as it allowed the ship to be more resilient under sail.

Above the tenth strake the planking was held by only half the number of ribs as below it. The fourteenth strake was also thicker as it had to take the weight and pressure of the oars.

Above the waterline the strakes were riveted, not lashed. To strengthen the ship when sailing heeled over, oak knees were riveted to the upper side of every crossbeam, extending upwards over four strakes, with two more strakes nailed to the top ribs above the knees, taking the ship up to its full height. The gunwale itself took the weight of the attached shield-rack, with space for 32 per side, two for each oarhole, each hanging overlapping the other and used for decorative purposes only, when the ship was not under way. The crossbeams were then laid across the ship from top to top of the ribs, on each side, and they finally completed the lateral strengthening of the ship.

A vital part of the Gokstad ship was the kerling, or crone, a large block of solid oak for holding the mast and protecting the ship from the terrific pressures exerted on the frame while under sail. This rested on the keel and was secured to the tenth rib from the stern by two solid knees nailed on from each side, and by a knee on each side to the eighth and eleventh ribs. Brøgger explains further:

> Right in front of the tenth rib, and forward of the socket for
> the mast is a strong, vertically inclining arm, grown in one
> piece from the crone. The socket itself is formed with the

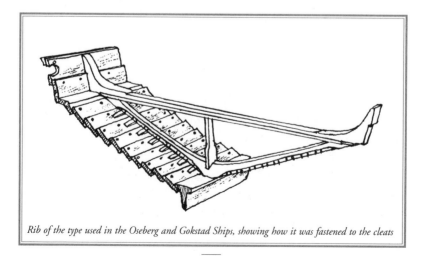

Rib of the type used in the Oseberg and Gokstad Ships, showing how it was fastened to the cleats

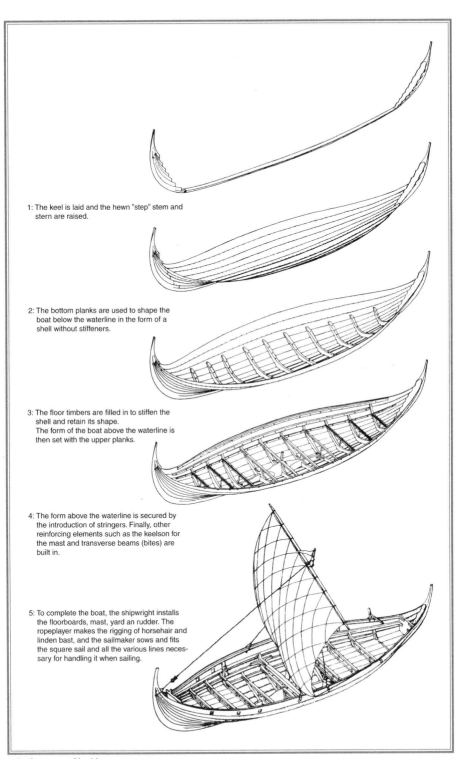

1: The keel is laid and the hewn "step" stem and
stern are raised.

2: The bottom planks are used to shape the
boat below the waterline in the form of a
shell without stiffeners.

3: The floor timbers are filled in to stiffen the
shell and retain its shape.
The form of the boat above the waterline is
then set with the upper planks.

4: The form above the waterline is secured by
the introduction of stringers. Finally, other
reinforcing elements such as the keelson for
the mast and transverse beams (bites) are
built in.

5: To complete the boat, the shipwright installs
the floorboards, mast, yard an rudder. The
ropeplayer makes the rigging of horsehair and
linden bast, and the sailmaker sows and fits
the square sail and all the various lines necessary for handling it when sailing.

The five stages of building

bottom rounded forwards so that the foot of the mast slips into place when the mast is raised, while aft it is cut square, to hold the mast securely when the ship is under sail.

The crone carries the weight of the mast and holds it firmly in place. The mast-partner (or mast-fish) is laid over the crossbeams, bracing the mast when it is in an upright position. The mast-partner in the Gokstad ship was huge, and the largest single item in the whole vessel. It was 5m long and lay over five crossbeams, 1m wide and 42cm thick,

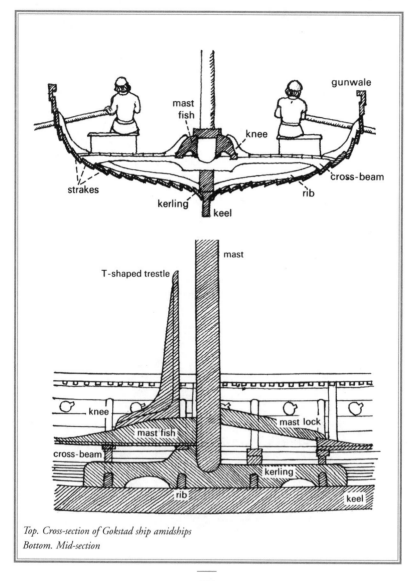

Top. Cross-section of Gokstad ship amidships
Bottom. Mid-section

Actual mast-partner/-fish

steeply arched and sloping down at each end like a fish tail – hence 'mast-fish'. It was firmly secured on all sides.

The slot in the mast-partner ran on naturally into that in the kerling so that the mast could easily be raised or taken down. When the mast was in the upright position it could be locked there with an oak block.

The other major problem with early Norwegian ships was the rudder which, of course, had originally been a loose steering oar slung over the starboard aft gunwale, and very difficult to control. The Gokstad ship's builder overcame this difficulty by securing the middle of the rudder to the ship's side. The rudder blade was fixed, in an upright position, to the rudder apparatus, which had to be extremely strong and was usually constructed from a large oak tree trunk. The latter was reduced in thickness to that of a heavy board, which was firmly attached to the inside of the hull, along the shield rack, and lying, from the last rib aft on the starboard side towards the stern.

The gunwale was reinforced where the rudder rested against it, and a heavy oak block kept the rudder upright. This block was held in position by rivets right through the planking. The rudder was secured to the ship's side by a long, thick withy knotted on the outside and threaded through holes in the rudder, block, planking and rib, and made fast inboard through three holes in the rudder rib. The pliable

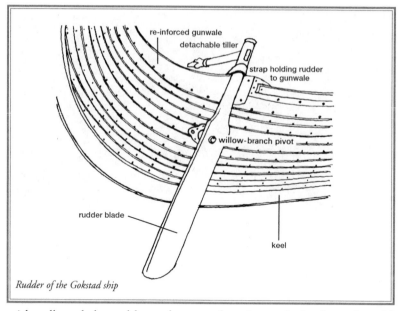

re-inforced gunwale
detachable tiller
strap holding rudder
to gunwale
willow-branch pivot
rudder blade
keel

Rudder of the Gokstad ship

withy allowed the rudder to be turned on its vertical axis, and could also be loosened easily in order to swing the rudder up out of the water when beaching the ship. This was done by means of a rope attached to the foot of the rudder blade. When in position the rudder hung about 50cm deeper than the keel, thus increasing the manoeuvrability of the ship. To keep the rudder in an upright position at the gunwale a strap was passed round the top and fastened tightly to the rudder rib. This could easily be untied during beaching. The 1m long tiller projected horizontally from a slit in the upper rudder and lay inboard, at right angles, across the gunwale. The floorboards of the ship were not nailed down but left lying loose so that gear and weapons could be stowed below them and recovered easily. They were laid higher at the stern above the rudder rib, thus forming a poop deck where the steersman stood with the rudder at a convenient height in front of him.

The mast of the Gokstad ship was made of pine, 30cm thick. It was the custom to have the mast length equal to the circumference of the ship at the beam, so it should have been about 13m high. Three cleats aft were no doubt for the sheets, (ropes for controlling sail tension), running from the ends of the yard (a horizontally slung spar holding the top edge of the sail), to the gunwales. As there was no cleat on the mast to hold the halyard (for hauling up the large, square sail), it may be assumed that it was fastened aft and used to brace the mast. The yard was probably held against the mast by a wooden hoop. There are

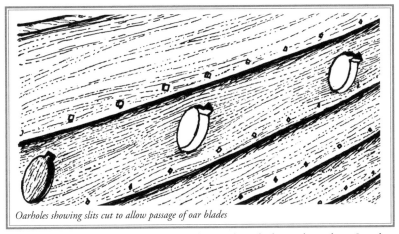

Oarholes showing slits cut to allow passage of oar blades

no traces of shrouds or stays on the Gokstad ship, though a Swedo-Finnish expert, Hornborg, says it was stayed right forward and 'sideways' aft, with stay and backstays. This was not unusual in ships where it was vital to raise and lower the mast in a hurry, and where the strength of the ship was in its oar power rather than sail power. Sailing was still an imperfect art in these days and rigging was probably fairly minimal. The vast kerling and mast-partner in the Gokstad ship were the obvious vehicles for protecting the hull against the considerable stresses of mast and sail. In any case, some seamen thought that an unstayed mast was more flexible than a stayed one, and therefore preferable.

The long, narrow shape of the ship's hull showed that it was fundamentally a rowing ship. The gunwales were parallel to the water line so that oars could be used throughout its length, and there was one rowlock to each pair of ribs, giving the right amount of space for an oarstroke. The 32 pine oars were longer at each end of the ship where the gunwale curved upward away from the water. Oarholes were made with diagonal slits cut out so that the oar blades could be pushed through from the inside, out through the fourteenth strake, and each had a circular shutter which could cover the oarholes when the ship was sailing, in order to avoid shipping water.

It is assumed that the oarsmen were seated because of the position of the oarholes above the waterline, but there were no thwarts in the ship. Possibly moveable seats were used, eg the crew's sea chests.

With 32 oars being pulled hard in unison the Gokstad ship must have been a wonderful sight as she surged forward in fine style through the seas.

The Gokstad Ship

CHAPTER EIGHTEEN

Viking Ships and
their Descendants

The Gokstad ship was only the beginning of the evolution of true sea-going ships of the Viking Era. She was small in comparison with the great warships which were to be built between the years 995 and 1263. Her length was just over 23m, with a breadth of 5.2m. Her height from keel to gunwale amidships was 2m, and her estimated weight, when laden, was 20 tonnes – whereas the famous 'Long Serpent', built in 999 for Olaf Trygvason, had a keel length of 45m, was 50m from stem to stern, and had 34 pairs of oars against the Gokstad ship's 16 pairs. But during these years the average North Sea ship settled to about 20–25 pairs of oars – more manageable and much less expensive.

Other famous ships, besides the Gokstad, were the Oseberg 'royal yacht' found near Gokstad (built probably about 800), and the Tune ship, all of the Viking Era. Like the Gokstad ship they were also used as grave ships. But these three ships showed signs of the wear associated with hard use at sea before being placed in their burial mounds, complete with body and grave goods. This was fortunate as, in all cases, the ships had been well preserved by the surrounding soil, and after careful excavation, were restored and preserved for us to see and admire.

The Gokstad, Oseberg and Tune ships were of about the same size and much the same type – large, open boats with no fixed decks and no crew quarters below deck. The true longships and Dragon ships, fast warships, were all much larger than the above three famous ships, though built in the same way. Longships varied from the smallest, carrying 40 oars, to the fairly standard sized 50-oared ships, though those built for chiefs and kings were large, carrying from 120–140 oars. The Gokstad, Oseberg and Tune ships were not built for war, nor for long voyages, hence their modest dimensions. They were coastal vessels which would be anchored, or tied up, at night and the crew would have slept in tents aboard or ashore. The longships, on the other hand, were sea-going vessels.

A king or Lord of the Isles without ships would have been an impotent leader, as Gillebride, Somerled's father, found to his cost around 1130, and the possession of a powerful fleet was always a valuable bargaining counter in the politics of the Western Isles, and of Scotland, in general. In the west, fleets were more important than armies. The Viking longships were built, primarily, for transporting raiders, and not for taking part in sea battles. Being bigger and heavier than either the Gokstad or Oseberg ships, they were designed to be ocean-going craft, capable of sailing all the seas around Britain, and the Atlantic itself.

This statement makes all the more remarkable the tremendous sea battle off Islay on a bleak January night in 1156 between the fleets of Somerled and Godred the Black, as described in Part Two, chapter 14.

Ships of the Viking Era were sized as follows. The space allotted to each oarsman was called a 'room' and this was the distance between the ribs or crossbeams of the ship. Gradually all ships from the Viking Age onward were sized by how many rooms, or thwarts, they had. Each room or thwart corresponded to one pair of oars and four oarsmen. By each oar there was a seat, or thwart, so, eg a 25-thwarter had 50 oars. The Gokstad ship had no thwarts, 16 rooms and therefore 32 oars. This system of classification was obviously based on rowing craft, but in the thirteenth century ships became measured in 'lasts', ie, by loading capacity, showing that by this time sailing had become more important than rowing.

There is a lot of accurate information about ships in the centuries of the Saga and Viking Ages (800–1300), and especially reliable are the sagas of King Sverre and of King Hakon Hakonssonn, as they were writing at the same time as the events described. There is, in fact, what amounts to a shipping register of big ships of over 30 rooms, giving their names, place and time of building, owner and number of rooms. This is not surprising as wars and raids were bound up with ships, and land forays depended on the presence and support of ships.

There never was a single, standard design for longships as each vessel was uniquely designed and built to suit the owner's requirements, but the word 'longship' exactly describes the warships of Somerled's time. They were long and narrow in proportion, making them fast rowing vessels, as well as efficient sailers, and tended to fall into the second of three main classes of Viking ships:

The Great Ships, of from 30–37 rooms

The 25-thwarters

The small ships of under 20 rooms.

The Great Ships were the equivalent of modern-day battleships and in early times these became known as Dragons. The ship register names 16 of these, all built between 995 and 1236, when production came to an abrupt end. They tended to come in clusters, during troubled times, civil wars and overseas expeditions, but none was built in Somerled's time. It is likely that, in the Isles, his prestige warranted the building of a big ship suitable for a king. There is no record of an actual, named ship in this connection and one can only assume that he may have had a ship larger than a standard longship for his own use. Ships of over 30 rooms were enormously expensive, prestige vessels, requiring large crews and equipment on a grand scale, and they were not particularly effective in a sea fight. They were often difficult to manoeuvre, and if the wind caught them abeam on their high sides they could be blown broadside on to an attacking ship, making them very vulnerable.

The ships of 25 thwarts, called Twenty-fives, were the most popular, being much easier to handle than the big, heavy Dragons. It is probable that the second class of ships, those of 20–30 rooms, counted as the majority in Norwegian fleets especially the middle of that group, the Twenty-fives, which were the most suitable. As the twelfth century progressed the demand for ocean-going vessels for the Norwegian royal navy increased. Naval experts and professional shipwrights came to the conclusion that the strongest, fastest and most effective longships were those of 25 or 26 thwarts. Their seaworthiness was of the highest standard, and they were built for speed, manoeuvrability and flexible strength. Originally, of course, they were designed for cruising, but gradually evolved fully into ships of war.

The superb qualities of the longship as a fast sailing vessel were shown when in 1893 the 'Viking', an exact copy of the Gokstad ship, under Captain Magnus Anderson, sailed across the Atlantic to America, for the Chicago Exhibition, held to commemorate the 400th anniversary of Columbus' famous voyage. The Captain describes it:

We were able to watch the movements of the ship and her ability to weather storms – the bottom of the ship was of primary interest. As will be remembered, it was fastened to the ribs with withy, below the crossbeams. The bottom as well as the keel could therefore yield to the movements of the ship, and in a heavy head sea it would rise and fall as much as three-quarters of an inch. But strangely enough the ship was watertight all the same. Its elasticity was apparent also in other ways. In a heavy sea the gunnel would twist up to six inches out of line. All this elasticity, combined with the fine lines, naturally made for speed, and we often had the pleasure of darting through the water at speeds of ten, and sometimes even eleven knots. – It seems absolutely certain that in those days too they wished to travel as fast as possible, why else should they have taken the trouble to improve the structure until it was so perfect that not even the shipbuilders of our time can do better. – The fact is that the finest merchant ships of our day, those regarded as the best sailers, have practically the same type of bottom as the viking ships.

He then goes on to describe the side rudder as having the brilliant advantage of being able to turn on its own axis, thus keeping its position much better than a stern rudder.

The third class of ship – the smaller ones – were those of under 20 rooms, like the Gokstad ship. They were light, fast and very manoeuvrable, and therefore of great use during skirmishes at sea. Smaller ships of about 13 thwarts were very useful in sea-fighting as they were often used in groups to harry larger enemy ships, as a pack of wild dogs will harry much larger prey. In addition, their small size made them ideal for portaging overland.

All classes of ships required a constant supply of timber, oak being preferred for the bearing parts, and pine elsewhere. Four centuries of shipbuilding had decimated the oak forests of Norway and it was at this time that the once afforested Western Isles also lost their trees and then their topsoil, leaving many of them bleak and barren to this day.

The longships, then, were the ships which built and held Somerled's kingdom, and this design, with its thin, light planking, single mast and square sail, was to be retained and continually adapted by other Northern European countries long after the Viking Age was over. During the period from about 900 to about 1300 new types of ships appeared, with bulkier shapes, higher freeboard and deeper draught, all designed for sailing but retaining the main features of the warships, including the high, pointed stem and stern and the side rudder.

Nach Urramach an Cuan
(How worthy of respect is the ocean)

The MacDonald galley in the coat of arms is obviously a stylised one, showing a ship with raised platforms having the same functions as castles on land, at bow and stern. From these lofty decks crossbowmen could keep any enemy at a distance. There were as impregnable as a fortress and any attacking ship which came too close was in danger of being hauled in by grappling irons and held until its crew had been dealt with. The forecastle and sterncastle additions are a later development of the longship design and could in no way have been used by the Colla brothers as far back as the fourth century.

The drawing of the MacDonald galley cut into the mortar at Duntulm Castle, Skye, is an altogether different affair. The ship still has the characteristic curved stem and stern, and the side rudder of the longship but depicts a much larger type of ship. Although very crudely drawn it clearly shows three masts, the mainmast apparently supporting a large, horizontal yard, and what may be a lateen yard attached to the foremast.

The galley's design must have differed considerably from the longship's in order to accommodate these changes. This possibly places the galley in or around the fifteenth century, for by now the pattern had changed. The clinker style of shipbuilding meant that the overlapping planking was, of necessity, lightweight and flexible and this, inevitably, limited the size and weight of ships.

Over the years changes in ship design became possible with the

Drawing of the MacDonald Galley at Duntulm Castle, Isle of Skye

introduction of the new carvel technique whereby the planking was laid in, edge to edge, giving a smooth surfaced hull. Now much heavier planking could be used, and ships were able to increase in size.

This, in turn, necessitated taller masts which could carry more sail. Carvel hulls were now big and strong enough to withstand the increased pressures of additional masts and multiple sails and so the three-masted galley came into being.

The longships provided the model for the later Hebridean galleys which were the basis of power of many western chiefs in the centuries after Somerled, and long after the Norsemen had gone from Scotland.

A 'birlinn' is the Norse-Gaelic name for a galley or personal ship belonging to a clan chief. These ships were built to the owner's specification, were highly individualised and thus highly prized. The birlinn was often regarded as a precious living creature invested with the mystic, supernatural powers of a talisman, which could protect the lives of the owner and the crew.

The eighteenth-century poetry of Alasdair MacMhaistir Alasdair tells, with affection, the story of just such a special birlinn – that of the chief of Clanranald – which, in spite of the ferocity of the storm that threatened to engulf her during a voyage from the Uists to Ireland, brought her crew safely out of danger and into calm water, without hurt to them or damage to her own strong hull. When the wind and sea at last subsided the skilful islanders unshipped the damaged mast and rowed her into the sanctuary of the sheltered east coast of Antrim. It seemed as if the birlinn had taken on herself the role of loving protector of her crew when their lives were in mortal danger.

Another famous birlinn which appeared to assume the human characteristic of loving protection towards her crew was that of the chief of Clan MacNeill of Barra, and is commemorated in this song:

A'BHIRLINN BHARRACH

Latha dhomh am Beinn a'Cheathaich
Air falilo o-i-u
Gu'n deach bata Chloinn Neill seachad,
O hio huo faluo

I gun slat gun rachd gun bheairt rith
Air falilo o-i-o-u
Gun cheann cumail air a h-acair
O hio huo faluo

Steach gu Ceisemul an athair
Air falilo no rionaso
Far am faighteadh cuirm ri gabhail
O hio huo faluo

Fion o oidhche gus an latha
Falio hu o-i-o-u
Is clarsach bhinn 'ga gleusadh mar-ris
O hio huo faluo

TRADITIONAL

THE BARRA BIRLINN

One day when I was on the Misty Mountain
Air falilo o-i-u
Clan MacNeil's ship went past
O hio huo faluo

It was without stay, yard or shroud to it
Air falilo o-i-o-u
Without holding point on its anchor
O hio huo faluo

In to Ciosmul of their father (it came)
Air falilo no rionaso
Where a feast would be got for its taking
O hio huo faluo

Wine from night until day
Falio hu o-i-o-u
And a melodious harp being tuned along with it
O hio huo faluo

TRANSLATED BY MR MURDO MACLEOD,
INVERNESS

PART FOUR

The Legacies of Somerled

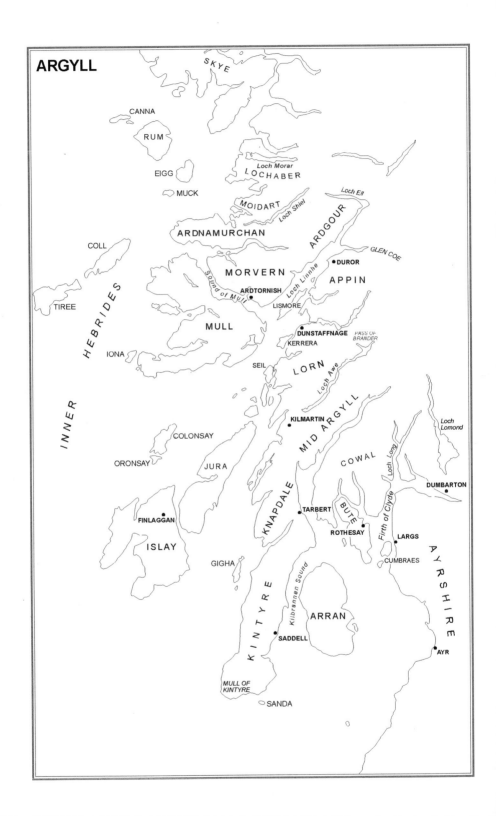

CHAPTER NINETEEN

Argyll and the Hebrides

After Somerled's death the integrity of his kingdom held. The Celts, far from being submerged, maintained their presence, and the Norse eventually withdrew. The later strong Gaelic resurgence which almost wiped out all Norse influence in the west, apart from the legacies of language and shipping, was undoubtedly due to Somerled MacGillebride, who can truly be regarded as the greatest leader of Gaelic Scotland after King Kenneth MacAlpin.

By 1164 Scotland had most certainly not become a mere extension of Norway – it was neither controlled by the Norwegians as part of Norway itself, nor as an independent country in the west. On the contrary, Argyll and the Isles was a unified kingdom, and respected, if not feared, by all the factions previously mentioned in Part One – the kings of Scotland, Norway, England and Ireland, the rulers of Man, Galloway, Dublin, the Orkneys and Innse-Gall, and the Celtic Rì.

Certainly, Somerled's catastrophic defeat and death at Bargarran might have been expected to lay his widespread kingdom, broken now and leaderless, open to inundation by the Norse, the Scots or the English. The islands north of Ardnamurchan returned to Godred, king of Man, under Norwegian suzerainty, as had been agreed after the sea-battle off Islay in 1156, but the southern islands were retained by Somerled's three sons.

In accordance with the ancient Law of Gavelkind, Somerled's kingdom was now divided into three parts among his sons, Dugall or Dougal, Reginald or Ranald and Angus, and so was no longer an entity under the control of one man. The Law of Gavelkind specified the division of land among the nearest blood relations of the king, (Somerled latterly having been regarded as king of Argyll) regardless of whoever was the eldest. Obviously each son was much less powerful individually than Somerled had been, and the unity and safety of the territories depended very much on how well each brother got on with the others.

There is little agreement about which brother was the eldest, but all agree that Angus was the youngest. The division of land gives no indication as to whether Dugall or Reginald was the eldest of the three, and historians seem unable to agree on the exact land division. It certainly wasn't a matter of the eldest getting the most or the best land, for both Dugall and Reginald seem to have done equally well in that regard.

WF Skene says that Dugall got Lorn, Morvern and Mull, but later changes it to Lorn and Argyll (ie modern Mid-Argyll). A MacBain, editor of Skene's *The Highlanders of Scotland*, 1902, agrees with him but his comments are not helpful as he didn't know Argyll at all well. Hugh MacDonald, the Sleat historian, gives Dugall Lorn only. Donald Gregory, author of *The History of the Western Highlands of Scotland 1881*, gives him Mull, Coll, Tiree and Jura. Domhnall MacEacharna, author of *The Lands of the Lordship 1976*, gives him Lorn and the Isles. AMW Stirling quotes Lady MacDonald of the Isles in giving Dugall Lorn, Mull and Jura. *The Clan Donald* authors don't commit themselves. Nor does IF Grant, who merely states that all three sons retained possession of Somerled's lands.

It might be easier to sum it all up by saying Dugall received mainly mainland territories and Mull, and Reginald received mainly insular territories, in particular, Islay and Jura, as well as Kintyre. Angus is either not mentioned, or is referred to vaguely as having been given most of the rest, or perhaps Arran or Bute and Skye, but, in any case, he and his three sons departed from the scene in 1210 when all of them were killed on Skye.

We can assume, roughly, what Dugall and Reginald received, by the titles used by their immediate descendants. Dugall's son, Duncan, used the title de Ergadia (of Argyll) and Lord of Lorn, later descendants styling themselves Lords of Lorn, while Reginald's grandson, Angus Mòr, called himself de Insulis (of the Isles) and Lord of Islay, later descendants becoming Lords of the Isles.

From the Celtic point of view regarding inheritance it didn't much matter whether Dugall or Reginald was the eldest, though there was a certain amount of status attached to primogeniture, as the Tanist system gave no good reason for passing over the eldest son, unless he were not up to the job.

The important thing was that in spite of the division of Somerled's kingdom the unthinkable did not happen – there was no immediate invasion of Argyll and the Isles by either the Norwegian king or the king of Scots, and neither the king nor his grasping Norman nobles got their hands on Somerled's kingdom. The family lost neither lands, prestige nor freedom.

It is true that the brothers were dissatisfied with their inheritance and the *Chronicle of Man* reports that in 1192 Reginald and Angus fought a battle, probably over the ownership of land. But, in spite of this outbreak, the brothers seem on the whole to have decided on posing no more threats to the peace and security of Argyll and the Isles by offering no further challenges to the Crown of Scotland. No doubt, in 1164, just after Somerled's death, they counted themselves lucky not to have brought down immediate retribution on their heads from the might of the royal forces. The ensuing years of relative tranquillity meant that Gaelic culture and identity continued the recovery and development which had originally been initiated by Somerled.

Political evolution, though, never stands still, and the twelfth century saw the Norse position being challenged by the growth of English expansion in Ireland. Norwegian influence in the Irish Sea was fading, and frantic attempts to save it by King Hakon IV were wiped out at Largs in 1263. This was the beginning of the end of hundreds of years of Norse aggression in Scotland, and the realisation of Somerled's dream.

The growing strength of the Scots monarchy in the thirteenth century finally completed the process when Norwegian interests in the Kingdom of Man and the Isles were bought by the Scottish Crown in 1266.

These events were to impinge on the newly divided Kingdom of Argyll and the Isles almost immediately after Somerled's death.

Malcolm IV died, in 1165, shortly after Somerled, and was succeeded by his brother William the Lion who, during the length of his 49-year reign, was almost constantly at war with England. This preoccupation left him little time for involvement in the west, for England, under Henry II was a divided nation, because of quarrels between the king and his sons, many of his barons, and the clergy, all of which weakened the country internally. The opportunist William therefore invaded England in 1173 in an attempt to fulfil the long held Scottish dream of the annexation of Northumbria.

It is noticeable that Argyll forces were not involved in this attack though there were men from Moray, Ross and Fife. This, no doubt, was part of the brothers' deliberate policy of keeping a low profile for as long as possible. For one thing, it was only nine years since their family had last directly challenged the authority of the king, and their loyalty must still be suspect. For another, they were not likely to wish to contribute in any way to a further extension of royal power which, if strengthened, might then turn its attention to dealing with the former rebels of Argyll and the Isles. It was a matter of out of sight and out of mind.

William's rash attack on England, again, in 1174, led to his ignominious capture at Alnwick and his forced acceptance of the Treaty of Falaise whose humiliating terms made Scotland a virtual province of England. So William turned his attention away from England, and became belatedly involved in the administration of his own country, but still he withheld his hand from destroying Somerled's successors.

A strange phenomenon was occurring in Scotland at this time. In the Highlands the clan system was becoming even more firmly entrenched – quite unlike other tribal societies which were becoming more and more centralised by the impositions of outside authority.

This was the situation in the Celtic North, and now it was William's priority to deal with it. And so, in 1179, he gathered a powerful force, invaded and temporarily subdued Ross but then had to invade it again in 1187, when he finally killed the persistent rebel leader, Donald MacWilliam.

In 1197 the North was in a ferment again – this time because of the Norse. Harald, Earl of the Norse-controlled Nordreys, had rebelled against his liege lord, King Sverre of Norway, and suffered heavily as a result. He then invaded Caithness in an attempt to gain what he could in compensation for his heavy losses, and brought down the wrath of the king of Scots on his head. Harald was duly captured and imprisoned in Roxburgh.

King William now looked to Reginald, king of Man, and considered the greatest military leader currently in the west, to lead a levy against pro-Norse Caithness, and bring it firmly back into Scottish control, so Reginald immediately collected forces from Kintyre, Ireland and the Hebrides for this purpose. Men from Kintyre could have been available only by the consent of that other Reginald, Somerled's son, and cousin of Reginald of Man. It is obvious, then, that Reginald MacSomerled was co-operating with his liege lord, William, at this time, though not actually getting involved personally.

Meanwhile, Dugall MacSomerled was similarly offering no challenge to the authority of the kings of Scotland or England, and we hear of his presence in England in 1175 while being accepted as a lay brother in the Church of Durham. The fact that this was an English, rather than a Scottish, church suggests that his presence in England was acceptable to the English king. Surely, therefore, Dugall had taken no part in William's abortive attempts on Northumbria. Nothing is known of Angus' activities until the open quarrel already referred to in this chapter, with Reginald in 1192.

On the whole Reginald would seem to have been the most important of Somerled's three sons as it was from him that the powerful Clan Donald and the Lordship of the Isles sprang. In a charter to the monks of Saddell Abbey he styles himself king of the Isles, lord of Argyll and Kintyre, a man of power and importance, possibly controlling more land that the mainly insular territories already mentioned previously. 'Lord of Argyll' would suggest the mainland north of Kintyre and bordering the southern part of Dugall's territory of Lorn. But Reginald was no warrior king like his father, Somerled, or his cousin, Reginald of Man. He carefully guarded the growth and stability of Argyll and the Isles, giving no excuse for interference by the kings of Scotland or Norway, his liege lords – a true grandson of that skilful politician, Olaf of Man.

He was not as devotedly pro-Celtic as Somerled had been, and the *Chronicle of Man* tells of his intervention in Hugh de Lacy's conquests in Ireland. He was well thought of for his many gifts to the Church. He endowed Paisley Abbey as well as the Cistercian Abbey of Saddell in Kintyre, for which he is probably best known. It is thought that he also founded the Holy Island monastery, off Arran, the Benedictine Priory of Iona and that of Oronsay, off the island of Colonsay.

The power and importance of the family is described in the *Annals of Ulster*, describing the destruction of Derry in 1212, by Reginald's son, who had 76 ships.

Reginald and Angus died in 1207 and 1210 respectively but the date of Dugall's death is unknown. The line of Angus died out as his three sons were killed with him on Skye, but his daughter (or granddaughter), Jane, married into the later royal House of Stewart. The lands of the sons of Somerled were, of course, again subject to the Gavelkind divisions, which later became the accepted territories of the great clans.

Somerled's descendants were from now on caught up in an

ongoing conflict against the remorseless expansion of feudalism throughout Scotland. They became the partisans of the resistance movement to preserve the Gaelic presence, culture and language which exists even to this day in the Highlands. Somerled had supported the Celtic cause throughout his life and kept his kingdom out of the clutches of feudal institutions as well as those of the Norsemen, but these same powers eventually brought about the downfall of not only the Lordship, in 1493, but the whole Gaelic system after Culloden in 1746, leading inevitably to the barren, desolate years of the Clearances.

But, ironically enough, it was that very feudalism that brought the kings of Scotland into the final, successful struggle against Somerled's ancient and bitter enemies, the Norsemen, and drove them out of Scotland forever.

At the beginning of the thirteenth century the kingdom of Man, and the Innse-Gall, were in turmoil again.

In 1209 some warring Norwegians including Ospak, a disaffected descendant of Somerled, plundered Iona. In 1210, according to the *Icelandic Annals*, there was warfare in the Hebrides.

The *Chronicle of Man* tells of a fierce struggle between two brothers, Reginald and Olaf, for the throne of Man. The islands, especially Skye and Lewis, were more or less involved. In 1224 and 1226 a saga reports that many of the Hebridean chiefs brought their complaints about this disruptive situation to King Hakon IV of Norway. There was civil war in Man itself, with Alan of Galloway joining in, and in 1228 the southern part of Man was almost reduced to a desert. Eventually Reginald was killed and Olaf became king.

King Hakon was not pleased, especially as the above saga noted that there was serious disturbance in the Hebrides and chiefs, understandably, supported either the one side or the other. Hakon was particularly incensed by those chiefs, descendants of Somerled, who had acted treasonably towards him.

In 1231 he sent a punitive expedition, under the command of the above Ospak, to subdue the west coast. Rothesay Castle on Bute was captured and treasure taken, then he attacked Kintyre, but Ospak fell ill and died so Olaf of Man took command of the forces. They returned to Man, then plundered Kintyre on the way north to Lewis where they obtained more treasure before sailing for Norway. As a result of this expedition, King Hakon's stature was inestimably increased on the western seaboard.

No doubt King Alexander was well aware of these events, but after an expedition to Moray in 1215 in order to subdue the Celtic rebels, and a reported expedition against Argyll in 1221–22, he became temporarily distracted by yet another dispute, in 1236, with Henry III of England, over Northumbria. Fortunately a peaceable settlement was made in 1244.

Alexander was definitely interested in reinforcing his position as sovereign of mainland Argyll in more than name only. He was admitted as such, although reluctantly, by some of his more rebellious subjects, as in 1227 he confirmed an earlier grant of tithes, from Argyll and Kintyre, to a Dunfermline church, and in 1240 he granted lands in Cowal and Mid-Argyll to Gillespic MacGilchrist, neither of which he could have done unless accepted as sovereign lord.

The 1244 settlement with England allowed Alexander to turn his attention to his next area of interest, the Sudreys, which evidently he was determined to recover from the Norse. A saga described how Alexander, a great king and full of ambition, sent envoys to the court of King Hakon making overtures about recovering all the territories that Magnus Bareleg had so deceitfully acquired from the Scottish Crown.

This probe marked the beginning of the end of Norwegian presence in Scotland, begun so long ago by Somerled.

King Hakon, in the same saga, replied that Kings Magnus and Malcolm had come to an acceptable arrangement as to the division of power in the west, and that, in any case, the Scots king had never had jurisdiction in the Hebrides, as they had been originally acquired from King Godfrey.

He then went on to reject Alexander's offer to buy back the Hebrides, declaring that he wasn't so poor that he needed to sell them – a polite but firm stand-off, which remained in spite of Alexander's constant attempts to wear him down. But Alexander was determined.

Other methods would have to be employed, and in 1249 he used a subterfuge to cover his real purpose of challenging Hakon's control of the Sudreys.

In 1248 Ewan of Lorn, great-grandson of Somerled, had gone to King Hakon to request lordship over the northern Sudreys, and also the title of king. This was granted, but was immediately followed by a furious charge of treason from Alexander and, as described in Scottish annals, looking for any excuse he deliberately picked a fight with Ewan, one of the most upright and well thought of knights of his realm.

In the previous year Ewan had done homage to Hakon for a certain island, as had his father before him, but wrote to Alexander saying that he would offer due homage to both the kings of Scotland and Norway, for his lands. Alexander retorted that no one could serve two masters, and received the dusty reply that it was perfectly possible to serve two masters, as long as they weren't enemies!

Alexander furiously gathered his fleet together and prepared to attack Ewan. He reached the island of Kerrera, off the coast of Lorn, where he was unexpectedly struck down by a fatal disease and died.

This shock broke up the expedition and left Ewan still in possession of all his lands, and still in the untenable position, according to Alexander, of being the liegeman of both the Scottish and Norwegian kings. The new king, Alexander III, was to continue a similar policy against Ewan, who was actually offered protection against forfeiture by Henry III of England, who described himself as the principal adviser to the king of Scotland!

The situation remained in stalemate until Hakon heard of vicious attacks by the earl of Ross and other Scots, on Skye in 1262-63. A saga reported that the king of Scots fully intended to take control of all the Western Isles, all of which made Hakon determined to reassert himself as ruler of the Norse empire which, of course, included the Western Isles. So he levied an army and left from Bergen in the summer of 1263. His large fleet of more than 120 ships, well found and fully manned, sailed to the Nordreys, then on to Lewis and Skye where he was well received, and on southwards through the Sound of Mull to Kerrera, where he divided his fleet, sending fifty ships on to Tarbert in order to raid and plunder Kintyre (no doubt to remind the Scots of Magnus Bareleg's exploits in 1098). Fifteen other ships were sent to Bute, which capitulated, while Hakon sailed on to Gigha. The Hebridean seaboard knew again the old terrors of a Norse attack. Many chiefs in that area, who were liegemen of both the Scottish and Norwegian kings, found themselves in a very difficult situation and chose to submit to the *force majeure* of the Norse presence, including Angus MacDonald of Kintyre and Islay, great-grandson of Somerled!

So far there had been no comeback from Alexander III who, like his forebears, had no fleet to match that of the Norse, and Hakon sailed on unchallenged round the Mull of Kintyre and up the Firth of Clyde to Arran. But Alexander was by this time in Ayr, ready to resist any attempted landing on his mainland Ayrshire coasts.

Negotiations for a peace settlement were attempted, without success, as Alexander said he would allow Hakon retention only of islands within the Sudreys group, but absolutely not the Firth islands of Arran, Bute and the Cumbraes, which were actually under Hakon's control while the negotiations went on. The summer was dragging on and the Norse began to suspect the Scots of deliberately delaying until the weather should get worse with the arrival of the equinoctial gales, because they didn't really want to come to terms. Eventually Hakon threw down the gauntlet and directly challenged Alexander to come to battle.

The Scots ignored this challenge, so Hakon sent 40 ships up Loch Long, from where they were portaged over to the inland Loch Lomond. As usual, the Norse plundered these areas and even rampaged right across Scotland before returning to the main fleet off Arran, where the waiting game begun by the Scots continued. But at the end of September the expected equinoctial gales sprang up, many of the Norse ships dragged their anchors and were driven ashore at Largs, on the Ayrshire coast, into the teeth of the waiting Scots forces, as had no doubt been planned all along by the prevaricating Scots. These events weakened the efforts of the previously invincible Norsemen and the Scots claimed a resounding victory – as, indeed, did the Norse. However, Hakon must have tacitly accepted defeat for he withdrew his depleted forces and sailed out of the Firth of Clyde, round the Mull of Kintyre and northwards for the Orkneys where he died in 1263. His great armada had achieved no lasting success. After his death his son, Magnus VI, attempted to negotiate with the Scots but, not surprisingly, met with a bad reception, the Scots accusing the Norse of having plundered and burnt more than a third of Scotland. But by now both sides were weary of the endless struggle.

After unmistakable signals from Alexander, in the shape of troop movements into Caithness, and fleet movements into the Hebrides and Man, the Norse realised that they couldn't keep hold of the Sudreys without a large, expensive force stationed permanently in the islands. In any case the Sudreys were manifestly situated in Scottish waters, and now too difficult to control against the remorseless, centralising power of the Scottish kings. This led finally to the formal peace treaty of 1266 at Perth between Scotland and Norway as equals, the terms of which agreed on the cession of the Sudreys and the Isle of Man to Scotland, in perpetuity.

The last vestiges of Norse power were removed in 1468 and 1469, when the Orkneys and then the Shetlands were formally ceded to Scotland.

The process begun by Somerled over three hundred years before, had come to its successful conclusion.

CHAPTER TWENTY

Language and Culture

*T*he *Clan Donald* authors describe Somerled as the saviour of the Gaelic language from the overwhelming Teutonic influence of the Norse, and declare that, because of him, Celtic culture and tradition received a new lease of life.

During the Viking Era, the Norse on the western seaboard had, inevitably, mingled and intermarried with Celts. Eventually whole families sailed in the other direction – to the Faroes, Iceland, Norway and Denmark, and then to Canada and America. Meanwhile, the Norse influence remained in Scotland but did not manage to submerge the Gaelic language and institutions. In many cases, after the exit of the Norse, their language died out and was replaced by a new wave of Gaelic, while in others the cultures and languages remained intermingled.

Even today the Norse influence is still noticeable, especially in the Outer Hebrides where there is a ratio of four Norse words to one Gaelic, and place and personal names retain their Norse flavour. The Isles regard themselves nowadays as the Gaelic heartland, although the formerly Pictish Aberdeenshire and Perthshire retain more truly Gaelic names than, for example, Lewis.

Investigation into the islanders' blood groups show close similarity to those found on Norway's west coasts, and no doubt modern DNA testing will corroborate these findings.

The ratios repeated here (see Chapter 3: The Norse Kingdom of Man and the Isles) refer to the period after the Viking Era with, as expected, the heaviest influx of the Norse language in Lewis in the Innse-Gall. The origins of local names show that in Lewis there are four Norse to one Gaelic; in Islay, one Norse to two Gaelic; in Kintyre and Man, one Norse to about seven and a half Gaelic and in Arran, one Norse to eight Gaelic.

The following areas have been chosen as examples of the wide diversity of Norse influence throughout the western seaboard:

Lewis: – in the heart of the Innse-Gall was heavily 'Norsised'. All Gaelic names were swept out during the Viking Era, and present Gaelic names are post-Norse imports.

Islay: – in the centre of Somerled's Lordship, was less densely infiltrated, but it is difficult to distinguish between Gaelic names before and after the Viking Era, except for Roman Catholic religious sites introduced in the twelfth century.

Kintyre: – part of mainland Argyll, and showing the balance weighted more heavily towards Gaelic, and with frequent combinations of Norse and Gaelic.

LEWIS

After the cession of the Nordreys and Sudreys to Scotland Gaelic spread rapidly back through the Isles and the incomer Norse settlers now became 'more Gaelic than the Gaels'.

However Lewis has been left with an unmistakeable legacy of Norse and Norse-Gaelic names, which beat the native Gaelic by four to one.

It is possible to find out whether a place name is Norse or Gaelic in character by noting the way in which compound nouns are combined into the name.

The simplest explanation is that both Norse and English put the adjective before the noun, whereas Gaelic puts it after.

Gaelic puts the generic term first and the possessive term after. Note that Gaelic has borrowed some of the commonest Norse generic terms, eg sgeir (skerry), and dail or dal (dale). So, when we have Skerryvore (big skerry) and Dalmore (big dale), we have Gaelic origins; and when we have Hasker (high skerry) and Margadale (market dale) we have Norse origins.

Looking at ancient farm or crofting place names we see, from their endings, their Norse connections, eg:

-sta, from the Norse, stadr, (a smallholding), eg Mealasta, Tolsta, Connista.

-bost, from the Norse, bolstadr (a farm or homestead), eg Seilebost, Carbost, Skeabost, etc.

-shader, from the Norse, setr (a sheiling), eg Elishader, Sulishader, Marishader, etc.

The influence of the later immigrant Gaelic is seen in the

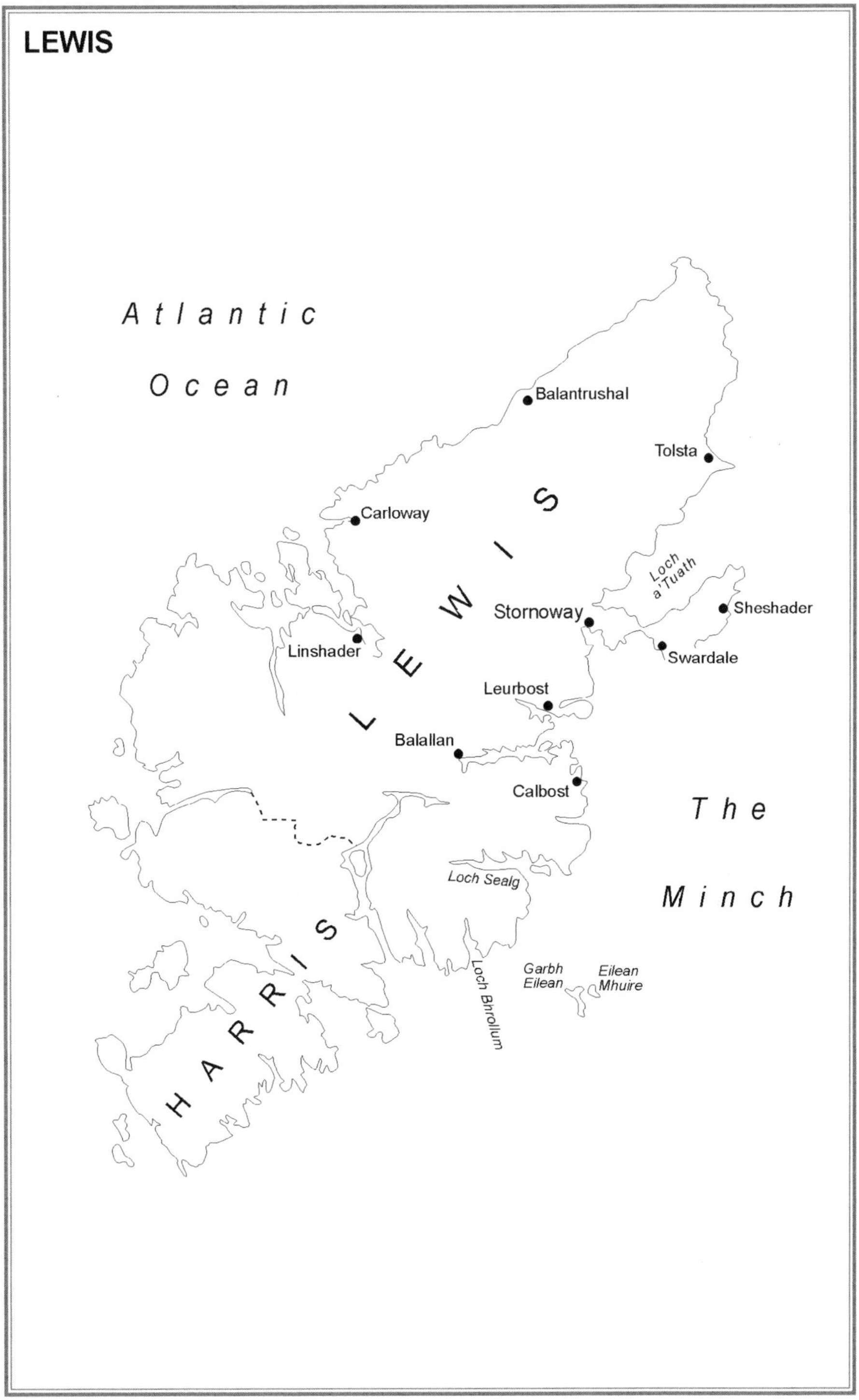

LEWIS

A t l a n t i c

O c e a n

● Balantrushal

Tolsta ●

● Carloway

L E W I S

Stornoway ●

Loch a Tuath

● Sheshader

● Linshader

● Swardale

Leurbost ●

● Balallan

Calbost ●

T h e

M i n c h

Loch Sealg

H A R R I S

Garbh Eilean

Eilean Mhuire

Loch Bhrollum

ISLAY

Atlantic

Ocean

Bolsa

Margadale

Finlaggan Castle   Balulive

Duisker   Port Askaig

Loch Langadale

Lamanais   Thòrrinis

Balole

Erasaid   Coullabus

Conisby

Dùn Nosbrig

Cross Skerry

Coultorsa

Glassansa

I S L A Y

Boraraig

Kelsa

Nerabus

Glenegedale

JURA

Ghaireasdail

Coillabus

TEXA

Stremnish

Gaelicisation of previously Norse names, eg Carloway was, in Norse form, Karla-vagr (Carl's Bay). When the Gaels retook possession this became Carla-bhaigh or bhaidh, giving its current modified sound of Carloway.

Purely Gaelic names now in the minority are:

'Baile', a hamlet or steading. This appears as part of a Gaelic place name, eg: Balallan, from Gaelic Bail'Ailein, and Balantrushal, from Gaelic Bail' an Truiseil.

Many loch and island names reappear in the post-Norse era, eg: Loch a Tuath, Loch Sealg, Loch Bhrollum, Garbh Eilean, Eileanan Mòra, Eilean na Gobhal, and so on.

Many personal names commonly seen in Lewis are derived from the Norse, though frequently show the returned Gaelic influences in the prefix 'Mac' meaning 'son', in MacLeod, MacAulay, MacSween, etc.

ISLAY

The word 'dùn', on its own, or as a component of a name, is early Celtic, meaning, 'a fort', and was in place before the Norse came. Islay has dozens of them of all shapes, sizes and ages. Pre-Norse examples of very small defensive positions, each just big enough for one patriarchal family are:

Dùn Mideir – Midir's Fort
Dùn nan Nighean – Fort of the Maidens
Dùn Glas an Loin Ghuirin – Grey Fort of the Green Meadow.

Forts built, or elaborated in the Viking era include: Dùn Nosbrig, from the Gaelic Fort, and the Norse Fort on the Crag, show the imposition of Norse tacked on to a Gaelic word.

Similarly, Dùn Gaidhre, from the Norse Godred's, and the Gaelic Fort, and Dùn Bhorreraig, from the Gaelic Fort, and the Norse of the Fort Harbour. But the Gaelic names prevailed, and were not submerged under the Norse invasion, eg:

Dùn a' Mhullaich Bhain
Dùn Fhinn
Dùn Mòr Ghil, and so on.

As the first Vikings came from the sea their arrival is reflected in the names of land features first seen from the deck of a ship:

Port Askaig – Ask Vik, or Ash Tree Harbour
Boreraig – Borgar Vik, or Fort Harbour.

Notably, many west coast Scottish names terminating in -aig or -vik, and including Ùig itself, shows the widespread use of this Norse word vik – harbour. All the -sgeir words refer to sker – skerry, eg Duisker – Dysjar sker, or Cairn Rock/Skerry; Crois sgeir – kross sker, or Cross Skerry.

All words containing -dail, -dal or -dale refer to a dale or valley, eg Margadale – Marketdale, Ghaireasdail – Gerdi's Dale, Langdale – Long Dale.

Words containing -ness or -nish refer to headlands (rudha, in Gaelic), eg Rudha Stremnish – Headland of the Current Headland. Rudha Thorrinnis – Headland of Thori's Headland.

The Viking raiders were followed by many of their countrymen who were farmers and whose settlements are clearly marked in Islay to this day. The words stadr, bolstadr, setr and boer, usually along with the owner's name, appear frequently as farm names in this list from Domhnall MacEacharna's *Lands of the Lordship*:

ROOT	NAME OF FARM	NORSE EQUIVALENT	MEANING
boer	Conisby	Konungs Boer	King's Estate
bólstadr	Bolsa	bólstadr	Farm (unqualified)
	Nerabus	Nedri Bólstadr	Nether Farm
stadr	Cultorsa	Thori's stadr, with Kula, a knoll	The Hillock of Thori's Farm
	Olista	Olaf's stadr	Olaf's Farm
	Kelsa	Kjaler stadr	Keel Farm
setr	Eresaid	Erik's setr	Eric's smallholding

NB 'boer' is rare as it means a piece of land too big for anyone but a chief or a king to own.

MacEacharna continues:

> The end of the Norse period was marked by the breakdown
> and disappearance of the language and the gradual assimi-
> lation of the Nordic peoples but it meant that, as the older
> generation died off, we were left with a large number of place
> names which had become unintelligible and had to be given
> a Gaelic dress. As early as 1385, the Norse name Texa had
> become Eilean Tecsa, Eikis Dalr had become Glen Egidale
> and Forsa had become Eas Forsa, or Waterfall River.
> Noticeable, too, was the emergence of the Gaelic word baile
> (a hamlet or steading) tacked on to the beginning of a Norse
> word eg Balole – Baile Olaf, or Olaf's Steading. Baluilve –
> Baile Uilbh, or Ulfr's Steading.

From the mid-1130s when Somerled held full sway over Islay, Gaelic
was inexorably on its way back, and although the Norse names live on,
Gaelic names outnumber them by two to one. Islay Gaelic, not Norse,
takes its distinctive place in the Gaelic dialects still spoken in Scotland
today.

KINTYRE

Although Magnus Bareleg and many other Norsemen, for their own
good reasons, regarded Kintyre as a Hebridean island, and therefore as
part of the Norse empire, the place names show less Norse influence
than do Islay names.

All the names, as usual, ending in -dal or -dale, -nis or -ness, show
their Norse connections, eg Borgadale, Carradale, Ifferdale, Torrisdale;
Stafnish, Skipness, and other names of land features:

> Amod – a plain almost surrounded by a river
> Àros – a river mouth
> Langa – a long river
> Tangy – a tongue of land
> Sanda – sandy island.

There are the usual hybrids, showing Gaelic reimposed on the Norse, eg:

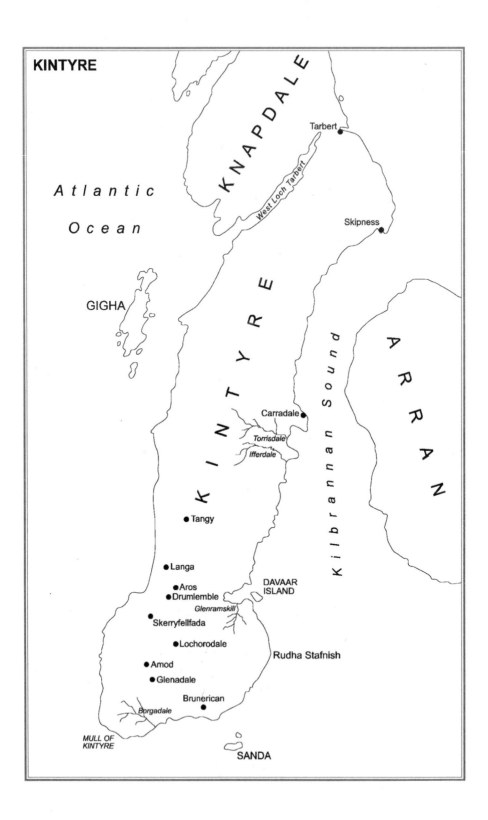

Glenadale, from Gaelic, gleann, meaning glen, then the Norse imposition a-dale, meaning river dale, reverting to gleann when the Norse had gone, but also retaining the Norse form, finally giving gleann-a-dale. Other mixtures are seen in Lochorodale, Skerryfellfada, Drumlemble, Brunerican, Glenramskill, etc.

Personal names taken from Norse derivations are, eg Caldwell, Langwill and Maxwell.

Gaelic ship words and naval terms also show their Norse origin, and have been retained, as has the Norse ship-building expertise:

ENGLISH	GAELIC	NORSE
anchor	acair	akr
rudder/steering board	stiùir	styra
boat	bàta	batr
rib	reang	rong

Hebridean crofters' houses, known locally as blackhouses, built of stone to a ground-hugging, rectangular design seem also to have been a legacy of the Norse occupation as they strongly resemble similar houses seen in Norway in the Viking Era.

However, generally speaking, and apart from the language associated with naval matters and houses, there was a steady Gaelic revival until the defeat of the clan system after Culloden in 1746, leading to the disaster of the Clearances when so much of the Gaelic language and way of life was swept away out of the islands and mainland, to the point of near extinction.

> *I see the hills, the valleys and the slopes*
> *But they do not lighten my sorrow.*
> *I see the bands departing*
> *on the white-sailed ships.*
> *I see the Gael rising from his door.*
> *I see the people going*
> *and there is no love for them in the north.*

19TH CENTURY BARD KENNETH MACKENZIE

In all the Hebridean islands, as well as the west coast mainland, the new threat to Gaelic was not Norse, but English. Even after the worst of the Clearances was over and security of tenure for crofters was guaranteed by the Crofters Holdings Act of 1886, it seemed too late – the damage had been done. The Highland countryside was seriously depopulated and the condition of the people was very depressed. Many thought that their inability to speak English was at the root of their troubles, and eradicating Gaelic became *'the thing to do'*. People of today, with Highland grandparents living at the end of the nineteenth century, and beginning of the twentieth, are quite familiar with sad tales of how even the smallest child arriving at primary or 'elementary' school on the first day, was punished for speaking Gaelic – although he or she didn't have a word of English! All during the school day it was strictly forbidden to speak Gaelic, and this rule was so rigorously enforced that most of these children learned their English with the threat of severe punishment hanging over their heads. They grew up with this policy of downgrading all things Gaelic, and the disparagement of the Highlands and the Highlanders was dinned into their ears until they began to believe it themselves.

Highland secondary school teachers, as well as many parents, insisted that, in order to *'get on'*, every pupil with any ambition in his soul had to *'get away'*. As all the universities, and most of the colleges, were geographically well away from the Highlands and Islands, *'getting away'* was indeed a hard fact of life for the young folk who wished further education, and, tragically, many of them never returned to their childhood homes in later life.

The deliberate eradication policy of the late nineteenth and early twentieth centuries was working only too well. In the 1960s and 70s Highland teachers used to say that Gaelic was still alive in a district only if the children spoke it in the playground, ie when unsupervised, and even in schools in the remote Western Isles Gaelic, in places, became submerged under English. This was understandable when there was a NATO base on Benbecula, and a rocket station on South Uist, with an international community living there. Gaelic was going further and further down. Enlightened people in education circles despaired of the language surviving even until the end of the twentieth century, especially when teenage native Gaelic speakers, right up to the mid-70s, found their own language and culture so at odds with the modern 'pop' culture, that they were able to speak, read and write Gaelic, but deliberately chose not to.

But there were a few plus factors. Some counties, for example

Argyll and Inverness-shire, had unofficial habits, rather than policies, of positive discrimination towards Argyll-born, or other Highland-born, teachers, and especially Gaelic speakers, right up to the middle of the 1960s. These people helped to maintain the language and culture under difficult conditions as there was still a hard core of people strictly opposed to all things Gaelic. Wonderfully, right in the heart of Glasgow (known as the 'Highland' city), there were two secondary schools offering Higher Gaelic courses.

By the early 1970s widely-voiced fears that Gaelic was about to become another dead European language caused the tide to begin to turn, cautiously, in its favour. Soon a bi-lingual policy was in place in Inverness-shire and Ross & Cromarty, though it stuttered in Argyll where only lip service was offered too often, and the common excuse of lack of money allowed unsympathetic council members off the hook of declaring a positive, official commitment to Gaelic.

In 1976 the advent of regionalisation saw the Western Isles separated finally from their mainland headquarters in Inverness-shire and Ross & Cromarty, and going their own way, positively recognising, encouraging and funding their own Gaelic policies.

Unfortunately, Argyll became a minnow swallowed up in the great leviathan, Strathclyde, with its heavily biased Lowland culture. Gaelic and the Gaeltachd were regarded as quaint anachronisms. Fortunately, within the great diversity of Strathclyde there were many 'exiled' Gaels, some of whom had access to educational and political high places, and a gradual, slow resurgence began, eg, with the appearance of the very successful Gaelic Language Playgroup Scheme, and informal Gaelic language evening classes and primary school classes, wherever suitable teachers could be found. By the 1980s mainland Argyll, unfortunately, had Gaelic teachers only in Oban district; none in Kintyre, Knapdale or Mid-Argyll, and only one in Cowal (at Strachur), though a sympathetic Primary Adviser did her best to arrange fairly regular Gaelic in-service training for suitable teachers.

In the 1990s, the situation steadily improved much more with widespread provision in primary and secondary schools, including the old Gaeltachd of Perthshire, and areas of the previously non-Gaelic speaking Lowlands. Gaelic was now classed as a 'modern language' and funded as such. The City of Glasgow has a Gaelic Unit within Hillpark Secondary School where most subjects are taught through the medium of Gaelic.

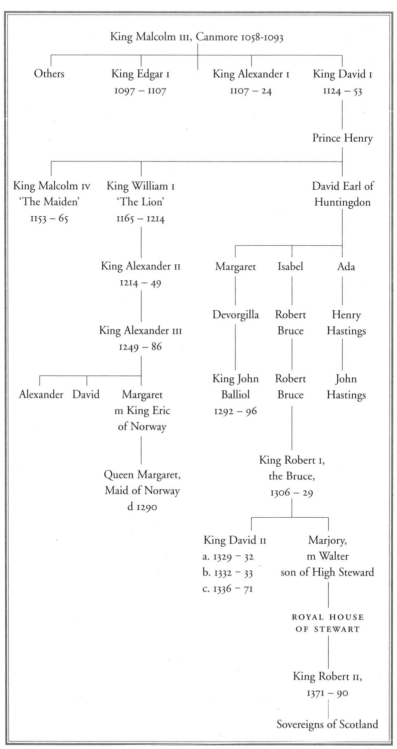

King Malcolm III, Canmore 1058-1093

Others — King Edgar I 1097 – 1107 — King Alexander I 1107 – 24 — King David I 1124 – 53

Prince Henry

King Malcolm IV 'The Maiden' 1153 – 65 — King William I 'The Lion' 1165 – 1214 — David Earl of Huntingdon

King Alexander II 1214 – 49

Margaret — Isabel — Ada

Devorgilla — Robert Bruce — Henry Hastings

King Alexander III 1249 – 86

King John Balliol 1292 – 96 — Robert Bruce — John Hastings

Alexander — David — Margaret m King Eric of Norway

Queen Margaret, Maid of Norway d 1290

King Robert I, the Bruce, 1306 – 29

King David II a. 1329 – 32 b. 1332 – 33 c. 1336 – 71 — Marjory, m Walter son of High Steward

ROYAL HOUSE OF STEWART

King Robert II, 1371 – 90

Sovereigns of Scotland

The Royal Houses of Scotland

Gaelic street, shop and office signs are commonly seen all through the Highland counties and there is now a cautious optimism that this beautiful language, so recently dangerously close to extinction, may yet be saved. The once threatening 'pop' scene has actually contributed to Gaelic's growth in popularity, with the emergence of bands such as the immensely successful Run Rig and Capercaille, and their Irish, Manx, Welsh and Breton counterparts. There are pan-Celtic festivals as well as the annual Celtic Congress held in turn in the different Celtic areas and there are now daily radio and TV news, documentary, children's and drama programmes. In the 1990s its very own Gaelic soap opera 'Machair', now defunct, was set in a fictional Gaelic college in Lewis. This mirrored the real Gaelic colleges – Lewis College in Stornoway, Isle of Lewis, and Sabhal Mòr Ostaig on Skye – which have become part of the long-awaited Highland University.

Gaelic has now acquired its own esoteric status. It is the 'in thing' to be from the Gaeltachd and, even more, to be a native speaker of what is, arguably, the oldest Indo-European language still spoken in Europe.

It is a far cry from the new Gaelic recovery begun in Somerled's day but, absolutely, undeniably, *Tha Gàidhlig bheò ann an Alba! (Gaelic is alive in Scotland!)*

CHAPTER TWENTY-ONE

The Rise of the
Great Clans

After the death of Somerled the Royal House of Scotland proceeded, according to the now well-established system of primogeniture, through the reigns of Kings William I, Alexander II and Alexander III. The latter died in 1286, sad in the knowledge that his three children had predeceased him, and leaving the throne of Scotland in a most precarious position. His only heir was now his young granddaughter, Margaret, Maid of Norway, aged just under three, whose father, King Eric II of Norway, had recently lost his wife, the Princess Margaret of Scotland. Obviously he was now very unwilling to part with his little daughter, who was considered too frail to make the journey to Scotland until she was seven. There was, therefore, an interregnum during these four years.

In addition, there never had been a sovereign queen of Scotland before and many of the nobles were unwilling to accept this new concept, especially in a country where Gaelic traditions of succession were still strongly favoured, even among the incomer Norman families. In fact, Alexander II had named Robert Bruce, grandfather of the later King Robert The Bruce, as his successor, and this had been accepted by the Scottish nobility, before the birth of the future Alexander III, and the now elderly Robert Bruce was unwilling to give up his claim. In 1286 he gathered his supporters together at Turnberry, in Ayrshire, in order to promote his right to the throne. These allies included, among others, Angus Mòr Macdonald, of Kintyre and Islay, and his son, Alexander.

Unfortunately, King Edward of England, grand-uncle of the little queen, had dynastic ambitions towards Scotland, and saw a first-class opportunity of interfering in Scottish affairs without going to the expense of a war. His idea was to marry his heir, Edward Prince of Wales, to Margaret, and thus ally the two countries politically,

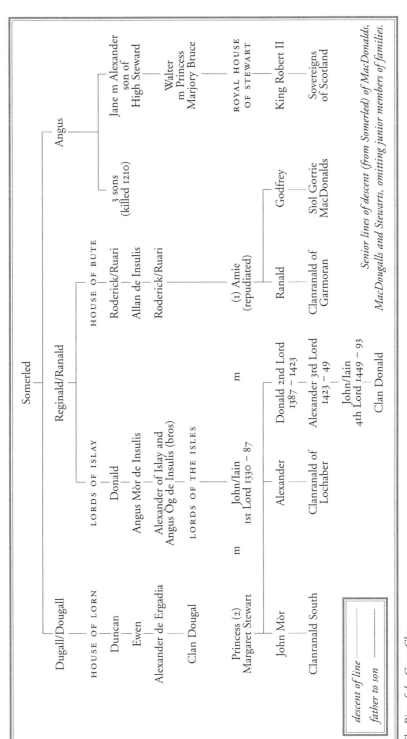

The Rise of the Great Clans

North end of Loch Awe

although he made ostensibly serious pledges to ensure the independence of Scotland. Naturally he was not in favour of claims from the Bruce family, or any of the other descendants of David, Earl of Huntingdon, and in 1290 he called the nobles of Scotland together to approve the marriage proposals. It is significant that Alexander, Lord of Lorn (great-grandson of Dugall MacSomerled) was considered important enough to be among those consulted. This situation, however, was aggravated by the tragic death of the little queen, in 1290, while on her way to Scotland.

The power vacuum which followed was to lead to the struggle for Scotland's independence and the eventual emergence of Robert The Bruce and the Stewart sovereigns. The death of Margaret led to the polarisation of the clans in support of the various claimants to the throne.

The major contenders for power in thirteenth-century Argyll were the rather obscure Campbells of Loch Awe, the much more prestigious MacDonald Lords of Islay and later of the Isles, and the MacDougall Lords of Lorn. They started out being completely absorbed in local in-fighting, but gradually became embroiled in the affairs of the state.

Being in the right place at the right time, and having the right connections is usually what decides who will ultimately be the most successful, and in the ensuing struggle the fortunes of the Campbells and the MacDonalds depended entirely on their relations with the top people – the sovereigns of Scotland and of England.

Inveraray Castle, centre of Dukedom of Argyll

At that time the Campbells of Loch Awe were a minor clan of little importance, and the Stewarts had not yet arrived on the scene, though their progenitors, the Bruces, were already eminent players in the political game. One would have expected the great family of Somerled, the Clan Donald, with their prestige and extensive territories, to remain the most powerful of the four.

The rise of Somerled's clan has already been traced. His descendants, the Lords of Islay and Kintyre, and later of the Isles, undoubtedly regarded themselves as of princely rank, and at times, the equals to the kings of Scotland, and in reality they were all powerful in the western Highlands. They had no scruples, therefore, about challenging royal authority, which, in the long run, brought about the unavoidable decline in their fortunes and the end of the Lordship.

In comparison, the Campbells were mostly to support the policies of the Royal House, and were amply rewarded for their services. Against all expectations it was the lowly Campbells, and not the great MacDonalds, who ended up as the prestigious Dukes of Argyll, whose status was such that they were able, eventually, to marry into the Royal House of Britain. (In 1871 HRH The Princess Louise, daughter of Queen Victoria, married John Douglas Sutherland, the future ninth Duke of Argyll.) This is not surprising as the Campbells, unlike so many other clans, consistently produced so many charismatic leaders, all through their long history.

The Celtic fondness for nicknames may have originally resulted in the surname, Campbell, from two Gaelic words – caim, meaning crooked, and beul, meaning mouth – giving Caimbeul, or Crooked Mouth, though the origin is lost so far back in history that this cannot be proved. Rather fanciful stories of a person surnamed 'de Campo Bello', who supposedly came to England with the Conqueror, have appeared, but not only is the name not Norman French or Breton, it also does not appear in the Roll of Battle Abbey, showing the list of knights who accompanied Duke William in 1066, nor is there an estate in Normandy or Brittany of that name.

The first name on the genealogy is, traditionally, Gillespic Cambel (usual spelling until the sixteenth century), who may, or may not, have had part Norman descent. His importance was his marriage to his far-out relative, Eva O'Duihne, daughter of Paul O'Duihne, supposed Purse-Bearer to King Malcolm Canmore, and of the line of the semi-mythical Diarmid, the Irish founder of the Clan. Eva, as her father's heir, inherited his lands on Loch Awe, and they descended to her and Gillespic's successors.

The Campbells had arrived. Their descendant, Sir Colin Campbell, who had been knighted by King Alexander III in 1280, and who had supported Bruce's claim to the throne, was very antagonistic towards his powerful neighbour, Alexander Lord of Lorn, Chief of the MacDougalls, who had supported the rival claimant, John Balliol. Edward I had been asked to act as Arbiter, and had selected Balliol as the weaker, and therefore the more easily controllable, of the two claimants. This initial rivalry, along with arguments over boundary marches, led to open warfare between the two clans in 1294, and to the death of Sir Colin, the defeat of Clan Campbell and the dashing of their fortunes for many years.

But soon the MacDougalls were diminished by the glory of the MacDonalds, and then, as events unfolded, even the great MacDonalds were to become almost insignificant as the Campbells grew in status to become virtually kings in Argyll.

Meanwhile the main dynastic struggle over the throne of Scotland was not resolved. Even the weak John Balliol, known as Toom Tabard or Empty Coat, finally rebelled against the continual, humiliating interference of Edward I in his business as King of Scots, providing Edward with the perfect excuse to invade Scotland as an outraged overlord. Balliol was thoroughly defeated by Edward along with his then allies, Robert Bruce and Sir Neil Campbell, son of Sir Colin.

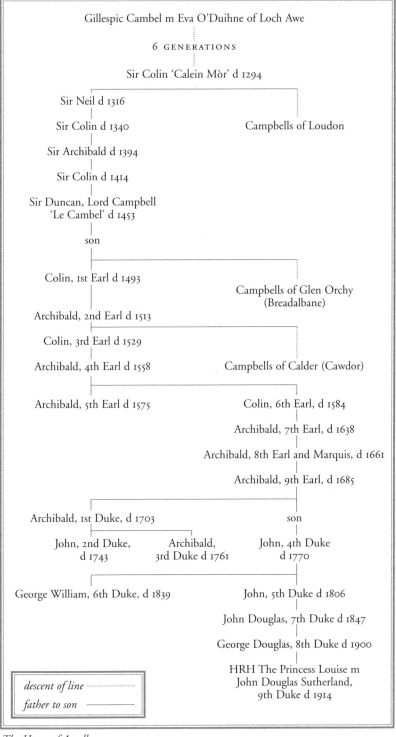

Gillespic Cambel m Eva O'Duihne of Loch Awe

6 GENERATIONS

Sir Colin 'Calein Mòr' d 1294

Sir Neil d 1316

Sir Colin d 1340   Campbells of Loudon

Sir Archibald d 1394

Sir Colin d 1414

Sir Duncan, Lord Campbell
'Le Cambel' d 1453

son

Colin, 1st Earl d 1493

Campbells of Glen Orchy
(Breadalbane)

Archibald, 2nd Earl d 1513

Colin, 3rd Earl d 1529

Archibald, 4th Earl d 1558   Campbells of Calder (Cawdor)

Archibald, 5th Earl d 1575   Colin, 6th Earl, d 1584

Archibald, 7th Earl, d 1638

Archibald, 8th Earl and Marquis, d 1661

Archibald, 9th Earl, d 1685

Archibald, 1st Duke, d 1703   son

John, 2nd Duke,   Archibald,   John, 4th Duke
d 1743   3rd Duke d 1761   d 1770

George William, 6th Duke, d 1839   John, 5th Duke d 1806

John Douglas, 7th Duke d 1847

George Douglas, 8th Duke d 1900

HRH The Princess Louise m
John Douglas Sutherland,
9th Duke d 1914

descent of line ··········
father to son ———

The House of Argyll

Tarbert Castle, Kintyre, built by King Robert I,
The Bruce, progenitor of the Royal House of Stewart

The inspired bravery of Sir William Wallace was not, in the long run, enough to finally end Edward's control of Scotland and in 1306 Robert Bruce, the son of Balliol's rival, declared himself king in a determined attempt to end English domination and fulfil his family's ambition. This was an incredibly daring act by a supremely competent general and determined man – very reminiscent of the great Somerled – for he had, as enemies, apart altogether from the ferocious Edward I, the considerable Balliol faction.

His gamble very nearly did not come off, after his defeat by the English army at Methven, followed by eight long years as a hunted exile. It was during these years that the friendship between Bruce and

Dunollie Castle, Lorn, stronghold of the Clan MacDougall

The Pass of Brander, from 1500 feet above River Awe

his Highland allies, Sir Neil Campbell of Loch Awe and Angus Òg MacDonald of Islay became firmly established. They sheltered and hid him, and fought battles on his side along with the Earls of Atholl and Lennox, and the famous Black Douglas. The MacDougalls finally wrecked their fortunes here by having chosen to support the wrong side in the struggle for independence. They fought for Balliol and against Bruce, the final victor and dispenser of lands and power.

In 1307 Edward I died, and his successor Edward II broke off the conflict for the time being. Bruce now had a chance of establishing himself securely on the Scottish throne with the unstinting aid of his old allies, Neil Campbell and Angus Òg MacDonald, though these two

Dunstaffnage Castle, Lorn

chiefs were taking a big chance in supporting Bruce at this perilous point in his career. It was by no means certain that Bruce would achieve his great ambition, so they certainly can't be accused of jumping on an opportunist bandwagon.

In 1309 Bruce mopped up the remaining MacDougall resistance, defeating John Baccach, son of Alexander of Lorn, in the steep-sided Pass of Brander on Loch Aweside, and capturing the strategic Dunstaff-nage Castle, which was then given into the control of the Campbells.

Bruce's subsequent campaigns slowly drove the English back into England where Bruce followed them and harassed them in their own territory, until 1314 when he returned to the only Scottish fortress remaining in English hands, Stirling Castle. The ensuing battle at Bannockburn resulted in the decisive defeat of Edward II's army, the unconditional recognition of Scotland's independence by Edward and Bruce's position as king of Scots no longer contested.

By 1314, therefore, the situation of the four clans was as follows: Angus Òg MacDonald and Sir Neil Campbell were well placed as favoured friends and allies of the now well-established King Robert I, The Bruce. In addition, Sir Neil had married Robert's sister, the Lady Mary, as his second wife. Their son, John, became Earl of Atholl, but died in 1333, leaving no heir. His Campbell kinsmen, however, received large grants of land in Argyll, along with confirmation of the wardship of Dunstaffnage Castle.

The MacDougalls' status was now completely diminished after their defeat by Bruce in 1309 at the battle in the Pass of Brander. They were, inevitably, dispossessed and most of their mainland territories were given to the Campbells.

The Stewarts were about to appear as the immediate descendants of King Robert The Bruce, and were to remain as the Royal House of Scotland, and later also of England, until the death of Queen Anne, the last Stewart sovereign of Britain, in 1714.

The MacDonald position continued to improve as a result of the gratitude of King Robert, and Angus Òg was confirmed in his possession of Islay but not of the whole of Kintyre. Bruce was a shrewd sovereign, rather like William the Conqueror, in that he tended to grant possession of lands, not in one solid bulk, but as individual entities separate from one another, thus slightly diluting the effect of the ownership of considerable territories. Angus was also granted the islands of Colonsay, Jura and Gigha, along with the mainland districts of Glencoe, Lochaber, Ardnamurchan, Duror and Morvern, thus becoming the most powerful of all the West Highland chiefs at this time.

But Campbell power was growing rapidly alongside that of the MacDonalds and, unfortunately, the friendship which had existed between Sir Neil Campbell and Angus Òg MacDonald did not continue among their descendants. Instead, the clans which had once been allies gradually became transformed into bitter rivals. Gradually, Campbell acquisitions in mainland Argyll increased until they began to associate themselves, as a clan, with Argyll, rather than with their scattered territories in other parts of Scotland, such as Fife, Perth, Dunbarton and Ayr, as described in *The Ragman Rolls,* a document of 1296.

This increase in prestige, of course, happened gradually, over many generations of Campbell chiefs, and right up to the early fifteenth century they were still by no means the equals of the Lords of the Isles, as the Macdonalds now styled themselves.

CHAPTER TWENTY-TWO

Lords of the Isles

John, who styled himself Lord of the Isles in 1330, strengthened the MacDonald ties with the Royal House by marrying, as his second wife, the Princess Margaret, daughter of King Robert II. John comes across as an astute, ambitious and not very likeable man – although known as Good John of Islay – who cynically ditched his sons by his first repudiated marriage with Amie Nic Ruari ('Nic' means 'daughter' in Gaelic) in order to obtain the territorial advantages of a royal alliance, in the form of charters granting the return of his family's former lands in Kintyre and Knapdale. The main advantage of these charters was the clause whereby the heir to the extensive MacDonald lands would be the eldest son of the second, royal marriage. This flew in the face of the by now well-established principle of primogeniture, but John got away with it.

The entire line of the Lords of the Isles descended from this union of John with the Princess Margaret Stewart.

John's first son, by his second marriage to the Princess, was Donald, who became second Lord of the Isles in 1387. This young man succeeded to extensive lands – more than any held by one person since the days of Somerled – as a direct result of his father's royal marriage.

At this point in Scottish history, as described by J Dunbar, author of *The Scottish Kings*, 1904:

> there was no law in Scotland, but the strong oppressed the
> weak and the whole kingdom was one den of thieves. –
> justice seemed banished beyond the kingdom's bounds.

And Donald, though a grandson of Robert II, who had been so generous to his family, rebelled against the authority of the current Scottish king, Robert III, and added to the anarchy in Scotland. In fact he regarded himself as an independent king within his own wide domain. When his younger brother, Alasdair, ran amok, seizing Castle

Urquhart on Loch Ness, and later burning the town of Elgin in Moray, Donald did nothing to control him, and Parliament demanded, in 1398, that both brothers appear before it to answer for their actions. True to form, Donald ignored the order, and considered himself free to parley with the English king, if he so desired. He was the head of a large Gaelic-speaking, as opposed to English-speaking, clan, and obviously considered the king of Scots almost as ruler of another country. There was not much that the king could do about the situation, and the growing rift between the Lords of the Isles and the Scottish kings was to continue from this time onwards. Then, in 1402, the earl of Ross died.

Donald's ambition was to hold the earldom of Ross, with its widely extensive lands, including the modern Ross & Cromarty, Skye, parts of Badenoch, Nairn and Aberdeenshire – a rich and prestigious earldom. Probably, to that end, he had married Mary Leslie, heiress to the Ross lands. Unfortunately, during the minority, and imprisonment in England of the child king James I, the regent, the duke of Albany, had had a similar ambition, especially as his daughter had, in fact, married the late earl of Ross. A clash was inevitable. The lack of any effective central government gave Donald the opportunity of challenging any royal or parliamentary authority in Scotland, by force of arms.

In 1411 Donald raised six thousand men and marched through the Ross territory by way of Dingwall, Inverness and Banff into Aberdeenshire. At Harlaw his forces faced those of Albany which, although slightly fewer, were better equipped. The battle which followed brought heavy losses for both sides, and both sides claimed the victory. At any rate Donald withdrew, and Albany was in no condition to pursue him, so Donald was able to retreat safely to the Isles, angry that his claim to Ross was still not recognised. However, there was no further trouble between the Lordship and the government until after Donald's death about 1423. But if Donald had won at Harlaw Scotland's freedom might have been at stake again – a politically divided kingdom, with two separate states controlled, one by a Gaelic-speaking leader, and one by an English-speaking leader. This would have laid the weakened kingdom wide open to attack from England, or to blackmail by Donald who would not have hesitated to ally with the English against King James I of Scotland. Alexander succeeded as third Lord, and in 1424 the young King James I returned from his hostage captivity in England, full of revenge against his hated uncle, the Regent Albany, and his son. No particular efforts had been made during the Regency to secure James' release, but Albany's son had been freed from England as early as 1402. Naturally the young king suspected Albany's motives for not obtaining the royal freedom also, at that time. And now it was a strong, determined king who intended to force his will on his presently lawless country, and who would prove to be no respecter of persons, however exalted.

By this date quarrels among the clans had escalated, and none more so than those between the MacDonalds and the increasingly powerful Campbells. In about 1425 John MacDonald of Kintyre was lured into a trap by the high-ranking John Campbell, and murdered. Although clan feuds over territory were common enough at this time the *Scottish History Society's Highland Papers* report that his death caused a furore throughout Scotland, especially among those people opposed to the king.

The king's advisers were scandalised at the licence assumed by clan chiefs, and magnates in general, and James himself was determined to quell their pretensions and enforce his position as sovereign of all Scotland. About 1426 he ordered the arrest of Albany, along with about forty other chiefs. Some were executed arbitrarily and others imprisoned including Alexander, Lord of the Isles. No doubt the king was stretching out his mailed fist quite deliberately. To the medieval Stewart kings the clans were always a threat to royal authority, and had to be ruthlessly crushed without any attempt at mediation or understanding. Unfortunately James' savage behaviour wasn't even justified by success.

Alexander, smarting under what he considered to be the king's high-handed conduct, immediately mounted a revenge attack against James, who furiously retaliated. Alexander found himself in the unhappy position of being deserted wholesale by former clan allies who had no desire to become entangled in a power contest with this strong-willed king. He gave up the unequal struggle and, appearing as a half-naked penitent in Edinburgh, threw himself on James' mercy. He was imprisoned in Tantallon Castle. The great Lord of the Isles had been utterly humiliated. Clan Donald was outraged.

One saving grace of his imprisonment was that he could not, therefore, be implicated in the subsequent revenge uprising by his nephew, Donald Balloch, who had taken over the leadership of Clan Donald in Alexander's absence. The Highland army unexpectedly routed that of the king at Inverlochy in 1431, and went on to plunder the clan lands of the MacIntoshes, the MacLeans and the Camerons who had deserted Alexander. Then Donald made for Ireland, to enjoy his booty. King James, meanwhile, had raised a new army and marched against the Isles by way of Dunstaffnage where he was met by the insurgents (except for Donald Balloch who remained in Ireland). They recognised the king's superior power and sued for peace, but James hanged about three hundred of them first!

Alexander had, by now, realised that it didn't pay to cross the king, and on his release from Tantallon, after less than two years, became a fervent supporter of the Crown, regaining the Lordship and the earldom of Ross, and becoming Justiciar of Northern Scotland – a strange reward for capricious behaviour – though Alexander did not get the earldom until after James' death in 1437.

After the murder of James I Scotland was once again plunged into a state of near anarchy during the minority of the child-king, James II. Alexander, Lord of the Isles, died at Dingwall in 1449, and was succeeded by his son, John, Earl of Ross the fourth and last Lord, who held great state at Ardtornish Castle with a semi-royal court. He married a daughter of Sir James Livingstone, ally of the powerful earl of Douglas, who, along with other nobles, seriously challenged the young king's position, during and after the minority. John became embroiled in this power struggle, on the Douglas side.

In 1451 James II invaded the earl's lands, and John sent the returned Donald Balloch to take the royal castles at Urquhart, Ruthven and Inverness, which he did, and held for the next three years. Although there was a temporary reconciliation between James and Douglas, it was in name only, as the earls of Douglas and Crawford and the Lord of the Isles were still in active alliance. The king's resentment flared into a furious argument, and led to him actually stabbing Douglas to death. For a time his throne was in danger, but Parliament condoned his action in 1452. John, alarmed by the king's violence, asked for a royal pardon and eventually received it. In 1457 he actually allied with the king against England, supplying a force of three thousand men, but James was killed by a bursting gun in 1460, and Scotland was under a regency yet again, until the young James III became eighteen, and took control of Scotland himself.

John's loyalty did not extend to the new king, and in 1461 he was back at his old tricks of parleying with the Douglas', and then with the

Ardtornish Castle

English King Edward IV, in a disgraceful plot to join forces and conquer Scotland. This so-called Treaty of Ardtornish, of 1462, planned the partition of Scotland north of the Forth among the two earls and Donald Balloch. They also agreed, upon each receiving a stipulated amount of money, to become Edward's vassals, and to help him in his wars in Ireland and elsewhere.

The Lord of the Isles intended to sell Scotland for his own personal benefit.

In 1463 he went ahead without waiting for English reinforcements, and sent his forces under his illegitimate son, Angus Òg, and Donald Balloch to seize Inverness again, where he assumed royal powers. The rebellion was opposed by the clans Fraser, MacRae and Forbes, and was short-lived, as John felt over exposed without English support. Edward, in the meantime, had made a truce with Scotland. For the next ten years everything went quiet, as, without English support, any armed rebellion was likely to fail.

It was not until 1474 that Parliament discovered John's treasonable activities of 1462, when England and Scotland held discussions to consider extending the truce to a permanent peace agreement, and previous secrets came out. In 1475 John was summoned to appear before Parliament to answer charges, failed to do so, and was unanimously forfeited. Earl Colin Campbell of Argyll was given the task of invading the Isles and pursuing John to the death – which he was all too willing to do – although it was a brave man who took on the still considerable armed power of the Lordship with, or without, the active presence of its Lord. But, in addition to Campbell, King James III, now approaching manhood, was himself bent on strong measures against the incorrigible John. He gathered together a large force to march against the Isles but fortunately conflict was avoided, and the earls of Atholl and Huntly are given the credit of mediating between the king and John, and the latter was persuaded to submit to James, as he had to his father.

Yet again, incredibly, he was pardoned, and did not lose his life, but instead lost the entire earldom of Ross, except for Skye, and his Knapdale and Kintyre lands, though he was allowed to retain all his other territories, especially Islay and the other islands. Possibly his fellow nobles, in Parliament, did not want to see one of their number completely reduced by a king whose power was threatening to become too great. John became ostensibly loyal to his sovereign lord who had recently attained his majority, and in 1476 the king ratified a charter restoring John to part of Kintyre, allowing him to retain his title of Lord of the Isles and confirming the right of succession for his two illegitimate sons, Angus Òg, and John.

There was peace, too, on another front. Between 1478 and 1481 there was a period of friendship between the Campbells and the MacDonalds, resulting in a marriage between Angus Òg and Isobel, daughter of the earl of Argyll.

But John of the Isles was now cowed by the king's will, and unable or unwilling to attempt to get back the MacDonald lands in Knapdale and part Kintyre. He seemed powerless to control the younger members of his family and his vassals, all of whom deeply resented their clan's loss of territory and the prestige of the Lordship. The result was that his son, Angus, was asked by the clansfolk to take over the leadership, and John was actually verbally insulted and turned out of his own house in Islay.

The endless strife which followed led to the first outbreak of civil war in the Lordship, for some MacDonalds supported the old Lord and some his son, Angus. The two protagonists met in an attempt at reconciliation, but no compromise was possible, and MacDonald fought MacDonald at the Battle of Bloody Bay, near Ardnamurchan, with a resultant victory for Angus. Unfortunately, at this point, Angus was maddened by the abduction and imprisonment of his baby son, Donald Dubh, by the earl of Atholl, and embarked on a series of rampages around Scotland in an attempt both to rescue his son, and recapture the earldom of Ross. This story ended with his murder, by his Irish piper, in Inverness about 1490.

Thus ended all MacDonald hopes of ever regaining all the extensive territories held under the Lordship during the greatest years when Donald was Lord. John, the fourth Lord, was now so feeble that, in 1491, Alexander of Lochalsh, his nephew, took over the leadership and immediately raised a force to seize the earldom of Ross – unsuccessfully. John was now forfeited for the second and final time on the grounds of having possibly connived at Alexander's insurrection. It was decided that having been unable to control his nephew, he was no longer fit to be Lord of the Isles. His ruin was now complete and irrevocable, and he died in 1493, almost unnoticed, after a career of foolish brinkmanship, disregard for opportunity and the gradual alienation of family and clan. The lands of the Lordship went to the crown. This was the end of the great line of the Lords of the Isles established so long before by Somerled.

This account of the Lordship, so far, has presented it as a political force constantly at war, if not with royal authority, then with other Gaels. But there was more to the Lordship than endless strife. There was still a close connection, during the Lordship, between the Isles and the north of Ireland, the original heartland of Gaelic literary and musical culture. The people of the Western Highlands deliberately adopted an Irish Gaelic culture, and an Irish origin was highly esteemed by the Scots clan chiefs.

From the time of Irish and Scottish Dalriada the culture, language and tradition of the Gaels must have been constantly in transit between the two settlements.

Irish bards and seannachies were honoured heads of centres of learning and patronage, not only in their own country, but also throughout the Western Highlands and Islands, and many Highland seannachies were of Irish descent, or had been educated in the arts in Ireland. If we can draw a comparison between the young people of today who strive towards the sophistication of city environments for their advancement, so the young folk of the Gaelic west strove towards Northern Ireland.

From the twelfth to the sixteenth centuries Irish seannachies were omnipresent throughout the Highlands and Islands. The *Annals of the Four Masters*, the oldest Gaelic manuscript held in the Library of the Faculty of Advocates, belong to this period, and show the literary and written language of the Highlands to be very close to that of Ireland, though it is likely that the spoken language was a Gaelic vernacular which, when printing was introduced, would eventually supersede the written version of the language. In Argyll the earliest printed book appeared, in the pure Irish form, in 1567. It was *The Form of Prayer*, by John Knox, and was translated into Gaelic by John Carsewell, Bishop of the Isles, who built Carnasserie Castle at Kilmartin, Argyll. Later books showed a gradual change to the vernacular spoken by the ordinary clansmen. As regards secular literature, the great heroic epics which have survived to this day could be heard both in Scottish and in Irish Dalriada. They comprise the legends of Finn MacCoull, the Cycle of the Ultonian heroes and the Mythological Cycle.

The most distinguished of the poets, bards and seannachies were included in the Ollamh class of Gaelic society, and along with judges, physicians and the most skilled craftsmen, held the highest positions at Court, next to the great chiefs and the Lord of the Isles himself. Bards were of great importance at a time of non-written, oral tradition, for it was they who were trained and entrusted to remember the Lord's pedigree, and to recite it, right back to Conn of the Hundred Battles, at the investiture of each new Lord. Most stories were in the oral tradition too.

Music was given a very high place in the culture of the Lordship. Martin Martin, about 1695, described the interest shown in music by even the lowliest folk. He noticed that very young children were able to distinguish one tune from another, and that each had his own particular favourites.

Long before the popular appeal of the bagpipes there was the clarsach, or small harp, which had such status in the Highlands that King James IV became patron of the harpists.

The professional office of Ollamh, being held in such high esteem, tended to be jealously guarded within families, and thus to become hereditary. For example, the *Book of Clanranald* refers to the Beatons, also known as MacBeths, MacBeathas, Bethunes, etc as being hereditary physicians to the Lords, having descended from the Irish Niall of the Nine Hostages. They were well rewarded for their undoubted skills, by grants of land in Mull and Islay.

The MacMhurrichs, or MacVurichs, were the hereditary bards, descended from Muireach, or Muireadhach, O'Daly, a Sligo man of the late twelfth century. Several of his poems are included in *The Book of the Dean of Lismore*. The MacCodrums were bards to MacDonald of Sleat, the famous MacCrimmons were pipers to MacLeod of Dunvegan and the MacArthurs were pipers to the MacDonalds of the Isles.

Art in the Lordship was spectacularly represented by the wonderful stone carvings of crosses and tombstones, to be seen all over Argyll to this day, and especially at Kilmartin Church, Oronsay Priory and Iona itself. This skill was cherished at Iona and continued up to thirty years after the Lordship fell.

Other offices connected with the Lordship show the extent of its organisation. The MacPhees, also known as MacFies, MacDuffies, and other forms, held very high office in the Lordship, virtually that of Secretary of State for the Isles. They were a Colonsay clan, and held the title of Recorder, or Keeper of the Records, to the Lords of the Isles.

Unfortunately these documents, either by accident or deliberate design, have not survived. The MacKinnons kept correct weights and measures, the MacEacherns were sword makers and the MacSporrans were purse-bearers or treasurers.

During times of peace, sports were introduced to keep the men fit and the Luchd Tighe, the Lord's personal bodyguard, were well trained in fencing, wrestling, swimming, running and archery. These skills were the forerunner of today's Highland Games, and feats of strength and daring were performed by these strong, active young men from the best families in the Isles, who were known as the Ceatharnaich, a name later corrupted into Kerns or Caterans, and used as a term of abuse by the Lowlanders.

There was a great expenditure of money during the Lordship, judging by the number of castles, forts and religious buildings to be seen throughout its area. The skills of masons, carpenters and builders proliferated during this time.

Another prestigious trade was, obviously, shipbuilding. Part Three dealt with the evolution of the longship, famously exploited by Somerled during his leadership of the future Clan Donald. The eminently seaworthy three-masted Highland galley evolved out of the longship and became the chiefs' main tool for keeping order throughout the scattered Isles, and for indulging in lucrative trade with Ireland, Norway and the maritime countries of Western Europe. Originally everything naval was learned from the Norsemen but, of necessity, the Islesmen must have become expert in this craft, and that of navigation, on their own account. Also the Isles were once rich in trees, as can be seen from the plentiful tree roots and peat bogs in the former Innse-Gall. Unfortunately the Vikings' and the Lordship's vessels, between them, decimated the timber for shipbuilding, leaving the Outer Hebrides treeless, minus their topsoil and covered with barren and bare peat bogs.

The Isles exported their traditional staples of fish, timber, linen and woollen cloth, flax, corn, butter and eggs. The spinning of wool and flax for cloth had been established in the Isles since far-off times. The Islesmen also built ships for their foreign customers. For example, in 1249 the French Baron Hugh de Chatillon ordered an Isles-built ship for his journey to the Crusades. Imports were wines, silks, armour, silver and gold objects and money. Nearly all trade was conducted by barter or exchange as coinage was scarce outside central Scotland.

The main power bases during the Lordship were, of course, Ardtornish, Dingwall and especially Finlaggan on Islay, and they must have vibrated with the life and the culture of the Gael. James Hunter's *Scottish Highlanders* describes Finlaggan in emotional terms:

> Here Scotland's Gaelic civilisation flourished confidently for
> the last time. From this place was ruled, by Gaels, a wholly
> Gaelic realm: a recreated and enormously expanded Dalriada;
> a conglomeration of territories which, at their greatest extent,
> included all the Hebrides, much of mainland Argyll,
> Morvern, Ardnamurchan, Moidart and the greater part of
> Ross-shire. Here Gaels, in a way that they have never
> subsequently been, were in full charge of their own destinies.
> No wonder that Finlaggan, in times when the greatness of
> Clan Donald was long gone, continued to haunt the
> imagination of so many Scottish Highlanders.

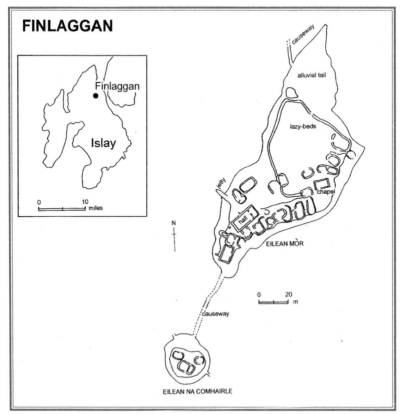

Plan of Finlaggan

CHAPTER TWENTY-THREE

Somhairle's Men

There is no joy without Clan Donald
No battle when they are a-wanting
First of the clans in all the earth
Each man of them is a hundred.

GILLICALUM MAC AN OLLAMH

Today Islay is a quiet green island, peacefully dreaming in the Hebridean seas. The Hebrides are now regarded as a lovely area, safe for people to wander throughout. Here we can take delight from the land and sea-scapes, the ever-changing light, the friendliness of the true Highlanders whose native speech is still Gaelic and whose soft accents make spoken English sound lilting and incredibly appealing. We can revel in the varying types of music, poetry and literature and the liveliness of dancing and sports. But we should remember that it was not always like this.

When speaking to the elderly folk of Islay one is struck by the wistfulness with which they refer to Finlaggan Castle, the centre of the Lordship of the Isles, the treasure in their midst, of which most were largely unaware during their childhood. They regret that it was disregarded and treated as of little importance, that it was in danger of being completely obliterated by the passage of time, and forgotten.

Fortunately, Finlaggan, and all it stands for, has been saved, and its importance as the hub of a vital sea empire, increasingly recognised.

Along with our appreciation of Finlaggan must go our recognition of the greatness of its founder, Somhairle Mòr MacGhillebhride, Somerled the Mighty, son of Gillebride.

Under his leadership Argyll and the Isles became a unified, Celtic kingdom, not an extension of Norway, nor an independent Norwegian kingdom in the west. After 1164 the integrity of his kingdom was maintained, eventually becoming the Lordship of the Isles. The Celts retained their presence, and the Norse were finally forced to withdraw. There is no doubt that other, outside events played their part in forcing the Norse withdrawal, especially the increasing English presence in Ireland and the Irish Sea, and the growth in power of the Scots monarchy, during the thirteenth century, but the catalyst was Somerled, and only he can take the credit for that.

He was everyone's ideal of a Celtic warrior king – full of courage and charisma – but, in addition, he had the cool organising ability of the inspired strategist, the fertile imagination of the opportunist and the ability to make men believe in him and give him their respect and allegiance. Without these talents he could never, in the face of such tremendous odds, have restored Gaelic sovereignty after three hundred years of Norse occupation, and handed down the esteemed Lordship of the Isles to his clan for another three hundred.

Apart from his undoubted military endeavours, Somerled's influence shaped the history of Argyll and the Hebrides long after his death, for he brought about the revival of the spirit of the Gaelic people of his own day, and rescued it from near extinction. Although the kingdom of Argyll and the Isles was divided up three ways among his sons, the two surviving sons were careful to maintain its peace and stability by avoiding any direct challenge to either the Scots or the English kings.

In their own way Somerled's descendants were partisans of resistance against the engulfing power of feudalism, following their father's example as the instruments whereby the Gaelic language, culture and indeed, existence, were saved from obliteration under a tidal wave of advancing feudal institutions.

Against all the odds, including, it has to be said, the apathy, and sometimes antipathy, of some elements of the Scottish people themselves, the Gaelic language and culture have survived – in spite of the apparent victory of feudalism over the Celtic system of government – and appear to be growing in popularity, especially as a focus for the increasing spirit of nationalism in Scotland today. It is probable that this would not be the case if Somerled had not initially rescued the Gaeltachd from the Norse domination of his day.

Somerled was the progenitor of that greatest of the clans, the MacDonalds, and also of the clans MacDougall and MacRurie. These, as did every clan in Scotland, tended to become confined to districts which became associated with their name. And so, by the seventeenth century, the descendants of Somerled became finally settled in Kintyre, Islay, south Jura, north and south Skye, the Uists and around Ullapool; the MacDougalls were restricted to the small area of Lorn around Oban, and the MacRuries had not any particular district of their own, but tended to attach themselves to other friendly clans.

The Clan Cholla, early forebears of the modern MacDonalds appeared, out of the black night of Norse occupation, as a shining example of what the clan system could be, and do. This was an ideal system, well suited to the times in which it began, and during which it existed, recognising, as it did, that the land belonged to the clanspeople and not to any individual, that the Chief was the father of the clan and its protector, and that each clansman was in duty bound to offer help and assistance to any other clansman who required it – a system which worked admirably in the Highlands until its destruction after the disastrous battle of Culloden in 1746.

The MacDonalds came to be overshadowed by the Campbells as regards the extensive ownership of land, but in prestige were probably always the first of all the clans.

Of necessity the MacDonalds clansmen became military people, and during future centuries were to become renowned as soldiers, the Highland regiments being invaluable components of the British army They were noted, not only for their physical hardiness, but for their pride in being Highland, their steadfastness, their loyalty and their strong sense of honour.

In actual numbers it is possible that the MacDonalds are still the most numerous of the clans, as an inspection of any Scottish telephone book will show, and their name features notably in the former colonies of America, Canada, Australia and New Zealand. Somhairle Mòr's empire has expanded further than even he expected.

As for the Lordship itself, at its zenith it administered territories from the Isle of Lewis and the borders of Caithness in the north, to the Isle of Man in the south. At this time Finlaggan was, without any doubt, the true capital city of a widespread maritime kingdom.

But let the last word on Somerled's Lordship come from the MacDonalds themselves – the authors of *The Clan Donald,* The Rev A MacDonald (Killearnan) and The Rev A MacDonald (Kiltarlity):

Considering the character of the ages in which they
flourished, it is not difficult to see that the influence of the

Lords of the Isles was exercised for the good of the lands
which owned their sway, and the terrible state of anarchy and
darkness which for generations supervened the fall of their
Lordship is alone sufficient to prove the fact. To the Kings
and State of Scotland they were turbulent and dangerous
because they never forgot the ancient traditions of
independence, but to their own vassals and subjects they were
kindly, generous and just, abounding in hospitality and
profuse in charitable deeds. Had this not been the case, it is
hardly possible to conceive that the Highlanders should have
rallied to so many forlorn hopes to re-establish the fallen
dynasty. In their proud independence they were to the
Highland people the representatives of what was best in
Gaelic history, who never owned a superior, either Celt or
Saxon. Only the king of terrors himself could lay MacDonald
low; such was the feeling of the devoted subject who
engraved the brief but expressive legend on his tomb,
'MacDonald fato hic' (MacDonald did this).

Bibliography

Adamnan, Saint, *The Life of Saint Columba*, publ Pengiun, London 1995

Anderson, Alan O, Anderson, Marjory O, ed *Adomnán's Life of Columba*

Anderson, Alan O, *Early Sources of Scottish History*, publ Watkins, Stamford 1990

Anderson, Alan O, *Scottish Annals from English Chroniclers*, publ Watkins, Stamford 1991

Anderson, Marjory O, *Kings and kingship in Early Scotland*, publ Rowman & Littlefield, Ottowa, New Jersey, 1973

Atkinson, Ian, *The Viking Ships*, publ Cambridge UP 1979

Bannerman, John, *Studies in the History of Dalriada*, publ Edinburgh 1974

Barrow, GWS, *Robert Bruce and the Community of the Realm of Scotland*, publ Eyre & Spottiswoode, London 1965

Bass, George F, *A History of Seafaring based on Underwater Archaeology*, publ Thames & Hudson 1972

Bellenden, John, transl *The History and Chronicles of Scotland, by Hector Boece*, Edinburgh 1821

Binns, Alan, *The Navigation of Viking Ships round the British Isles*, publ by the 5th Viking Congress, Torshavn 1965

Brander, Michael, *The Making of the Highlands*, publ Guild Publishing London 1980

Bremner, RL, *The Norsemen in Alban*, publ Maclehose, Jackson & Co Glasgow 1923

Brøgger, AW, *Ancient Emigrants*, publ Oxford 1929

Brøgger, AW & Shetelig, H, *The Viking Ships, Their Ancestry & Evolution*, publ C Hurst London 1951

Brown, P Hume, *History of Scotland*, Cambridge UP 1912

Browne, James, *History of the Highlands and the Highland Clans*, 1838

Campbell, JF, *Popular Tales of the West Highlands*, publ Wildwood House

Chadwick, HM, *Early Scotland: the Picts, the Scots and the Welsh of Southern Scotland*, publ Cambridge UP 1949

Chadwick, Nora K, *Celtic Britain*, publ Thames & Hudson London 1963

Chadwick, Nora K, *The British Heroic Age; the Welsh and the Men of the North*, Cardiff 1976

Chadwick, Nora K, *The Celts*, publ Pelican London 1971

Cooper, D, *The Hebridean Connection*, publ Routledge & Kegan Paul, London 1977

Craw, JH, *Excavations at Dunadd and at other sites on the Poltalloch estates*, Argyll, publ Proc Soc Antiq Scotland 1930

Crawford, BE, *Scandinavian Scotland*, publ Leicester UP 1987

Curtis, E, *The History Of Ireland*, publ Methuen & Co, London 1936

Davies, John, *A History of Wales*, publ Allen Lane, London 1993

Dewar, J, *The Dewar Manuscripts*, publ Wm MacLellan, Glasgow 1964

Dickinson, WC, *Scotland from the Earliest Times to 1603*, publ Nelson 1961

Donaldson, Gordon, *Scottish Kings*, publ BT Batsford, London 1967

Dunbar, J, *The Scottish Kings*, 1904

Duncan, AAM, Scotland, *The Making of the Kingdom*, Edinburgh 1975

Edwards, P, Pálsson, H, transl *Orkneyinga Saga*, publ London 1978

Ellis, Peter Berresford, *Caesar's Invasion of Britain*, publ Book Club Assoc London 1978

Ellis, Peter Berresford, *The Celtic Empire: The First Millenium of Celtic History*, publ Constable, London 1990

Fell, C, Lucas, J, transl, *Egil's Saga*

Foote, P, ed *Sagas of the Norse Kings*, publ Everyman, London 1961

Fordun, John, *Chronica Gentis Scotorum*, ed & transl by WF Skene 1871-1872

Fordun, John, *Scotichronicon*, ed & transl by WF Skene, 1871-1872

Garmonsway, GN, transl & ed *The Anglo-Saxon Chronicle*, publ JM Dent, London 1953

Gillies, HC, *The Place Names of Argyll*, 1906

Grant, IF, *The Clan Donald*, publ Johnston, Edinburgh & London 1952

Grant, IF, *The Lordship of the Isles*, publ The Mercat Press, Edinburgh 1982

Grant, Neil, *The Campbells of Argyll*, publ F Watts, London 1975

Gregory, D, *The History of the Western Highlands & Islands of Scotland*, publ Hamilton Adams & Co, London, and TD Morrison, Glasgow 1881

Grimble, Ian, *Highland Man*, publ HIDB, Inverness 1980

Grimble, Ian, *Scottish Islands*, publ BBC, London 1985

Gruamach, Donald, *The Foundations of Islay*, 1970

Gudmundsson, F, *Orkneyinga Saga*, publ Reykjavik 1968

Henderson, G, *The Norse Influence on Celtic Scotland*, publ Glasgow 1910

Henderson, Isabel, *The Picts*, publ 1967

Henry, F, *The Book of Kells*, publ London 1974

Hughes, K, *Celtic Britain in the Early Middle Ages*, publ Woodbridge, 1980

Jones, G, *A History of the Vikings*, publ Oxford 1968

Kenney, JF, *The Sources for the Early History of Ireland*, publ Dublin 1979

Laing, Lloyd, *Celtic Britain*, publ Book Club Associates, London 1979

Laing, Lloyd, *The Archaeology of Late Celtic Britain and Ireland* c 400-1200 AD, publ P Methuen, London 1975

Laing, S, transl *Heimskringla*

Linklater, Eric, *Robert the Bruce*

Loyn, HR, *The Vikings in Britain*, publ London 1977

MacBain, A, *The Place Names of the Highlands and Islands of Scotland*, publ Aeneas MacKay, Edinburgh 1922

MacBain, A, ed Skene's *Highlanders of Scotland* 1902

MacBain, A, Kennedy, J, *Reliquae Celticae, The Red Book of Clanranald*, publ The Northern Counties Newspaper & Publishing Co Ltd, Inverness 1894

MacDonald, A, MacDonald, A, *The Clan Donald*, publ The Northern Counties, etc Inverness 1896

MacDonald, Hugh, *The History of the MacDonalds*, publ The Scottish History Society's Highland Papers

MacEacharna, Domhnall, *The Lands of the Lordship*, publ Argyll Reproductions, 1976

MacKenzie, Agnes Mure, *A History of Scotland*, 1964

MacKerral, A, *Kintyre in the 17th Century*, publ Oliver & Boyd, Edinburgh 1948

MacKerral, A, *The Clan Campbell*, 1953

Mackie, JD, *A History of Scotland*, 1964

MacNeill, P, Nicholson, R ed, *An Historical Atlas of Scotland*, publ The Scottish Medievalists, 1975

MacNiocaill, G, *Ireland before the Normans*, Dublin 1972

McDonald, R Andrew, *The Kingdom of the Isles*, publ Tuckwell Press, East Linton 1977

Magnusson, H, Pálsson, H, *Njal's Saga*, publ Harmondsworth 1974

Magnusson, H, Pálsson, H, *The Vinland Sagas*, publ Penguin Classics 1965

Martin, Martin, *A Description of the Western Isles of Scotland*, publ Birlinn 1994

Menzies, G, ed *Who Are The Scots?*, publ BBC, London 1971

Meyer, Kuno, *Ancient Irish Poetry*, 1913

Morris, J, *The Age of Arthur*, London 1973

Mudie, R & C, *The Story of the Sailing Ship*, publ Cavendish 1975

O Corráin, Donncha, *Ireland before the Normans*, publ Gill & MacMillan, Dublin 1972

Pálsson, H, Edwards, P, *Eyrbyggia Saga*, Toronto 1973

Pálsson, H, Edwards, P, *Orkneyinga Saga*, London 1978

Piggott, Stuart, *Scotland before History*, 1958

Press, M, transl *Laxdoela Saga*, publ Everyman, London 1965

Reece, R, *Recent Work on Iona*, Scottish Archaeological Forum, 1973

Reeves, W, ed *The Life of Saint Columba founder of Hy written by Adamnan*, Dublin 1857

Richmond, IA, ed *Roman and Native in North Britain*, Edinburgh 1958

Roberts, M, *The Fury of the Vikings*, publ The Way It Was Series, Cambridge 1977

Sellar, WDH, *Family Origins in Cowal and Knapdale*, Scottish Studies 1971

Sellar, WDH, *The Origins and Ancestry of Somerled*, Scottish historical Review, 1966

Simpson, J, transl *Olaf Sagas*, publ Everyman, London 1964

Skene's ed *Senchus fer n Alban*, Dublin

Skene's ed *The Book of the Dean of Lismore*, publ Edmonston & Douglas, 1862

Skene, WF, *Celtic Scotland*, 1886-90

Skene, WF, *Chronicles of the Picts*

Skene, WF, *The Highlanders of Scotland*, ed MacBain, A, publ MacKay, Stirling 1902

Smith, A, *Loch Etive and the sons of Uisneach*, publ Gardner, 1885

Smith, CG, *The Book of Islay*

Smyth, Alfred P, *Warlords and Holy Men*, publ Edward Arnold, London 1984

Stirling, AMW, *MacDonald of the Isles*, publ J Murray, London 1913

Sullivan, E, *The Book of Kells*, London 1914

Swanton, Michael, transl & ed *Anglo-Saxon Chronicle*, publ JM Dent, London 1996

Taylor, Alexander B, transl *Orkneyinga Saga*, publ Oliver & Boyd, London & Edinburgh 1938

Thomas, C, *The Early Christian Archaeology of North Britain*, London & Glasgow 1971

Thomas, Thomas, ed *The Acts of Parliament of Scotland*

Vigfusson, G, ed *The Icelandic Sagas*, Rolls Series no 88, London 1887

Wainwright, FT, *The Problem of the Picts*, publ Nelson, Edinburgh 1955

Watson, WJ, *Celtic Place Names of Scotland*, publ Blackwood, Glasgow 1926

Williams, Ann, Smyth, Alfred P, Kirby, DP, *A Biographical Dictionary of Dark Age Britain*, publ Seaby, London 1991

Whittington, G, *Place Names and the Settlement Patterns of Dark Age Scotland*, Proc Soc Antiq Scotland, 1977

Pronunciation Guide

Guide to the pronunciation of Scottish and Irish names used in this book

c is a hard sound in Gaelic, as in English k
ch is guttural, as in Scottish 'loch'
u is a short sound, as in English 'cut'
g is a hard sound, as in English 'give'
phonetic symbol œ is similar to French eu
phonetic symbol ay sounds as in English 'say'
phonetic symbol aiy sounds as in English 'sky'
phonetic symbol tch sounds as in English 'church'

Somhairle Mòr MacGhillebhride pronounced Saw-ur-lay More Machk-Ille-vreej œ
Gall-Gàidheil/eal pronounced Gowl- Gayil/al
Druim Alban pronounced Drime Alban
Lochlann pronounced Lochlown
Fionn- Gall pronounced Fyoonœ-Gowl
Dubh-Gall pronounced Doo-Gowl
Gillebride pronounced Geelœ-breejœ
Gilleadamnan pronounced Geelœ-adamnan
Aodh pronounced œgh
Eochaidh pronounced Yochay
Righ-Fhionngall pronounced Ree-Yoonœ-gowl
Innse-Gall pronounced Eenshœ-Gowl
Columcille pronounced Columkeelœ
Suibhne pronounced Sweenyœ
beul-aithris pronounced bee-ul areesh
Dalriada pronounced Dal Ree-utu (emphasis on the ee)
Cairbre pronounced Carbrœ
Toiseach pronounced Toshuch
Uí Macc-Uais pronounced Ee Mac-oosh (Irish sound)
Colla Uais pronounced Colla Oo-aiysh (Scottish sound)
Tioram pronounced Tchirum
Eilean Na Comhairle pronounced Aylun na Caw-ur-lu
O'Duihne pronounced O'Dweenyœ
Nial/Niall/Njal pronounced Nee-ul

Index

abbeys 8–9, 85, 89, 123
Achaglachach 38
Ada, sister of Malcolm IV 85
Adamnan 13
Affrica Queen of Man and the Isles,
  41, 72
agriculture 23–4
Ailred of Rielvaux 71
Airgialla people 58
Alan of Galloway 124
Alasdair, Alasdair MacMhaistir 114–15
Albany, Duke of 153, 154
Alexander, Lord of Lorn 144, 146
Alexander, Lord of the Isles *see*
MacDonald, Alexander, Lord of the Isles
Alexander I, King of Scotland 8, 12, 13
Alexander II, King of Scotland 125–6
Alexander III, King of Scotland 126–7,
  142, 146
Alexander of Lochalsh 158
Alfred the Great 8, 9
Alnwick 122
America 99, 111–12
Anastasius IV, Pope 80
Anderson, Captain Magnus 111–12
Anglesey 16, 28
Angus, son of Somerled 119–21, 122, 123
Angus and the Mearns 32, 34
Angus Mòr 120
Anjou 21
Annals of Innisfallen, The 13, 16, 25, 43
Annals of the Four Masters, The 45, 46,
  59, 159
Annals of Ulster, The 12, 25, 41, 43, 88,
  123
Anne, Queen of England 150
Antrim 36, 115

Aodh, son-in-law of King Lulach 70
Aodh, 1st Earl of Moray 12
Appin 65, 66
archery 65
Ard Righ (High King of Scots) 32, 34
Ardgour 61, 65, 66, 67
Ardnamuchan 119
Ardtornish, Treaty of (1462) 157
Ardtornish Castle 61, 66, 155, 156, 162
Argyll 7, 8, 31, 32, 38, 44
  castles 63, 66, 67–8
  coastline of 13, 66–7
  David I's overlordship of 70–1
  division of land after Somerled's
    death 119–21
  Dukes of 145, 147, 150–1
  Gaelic language 138–9
  Irish settlements in 38
  Norse influence in 135–7
  Norsemen in 61–5, 119
  under Reginald 123
Arran 45, 70, 72, 120, 127, 129
Atholl, Earls of 149, 157
Atholl and Gowrie 32, 34
Atlantic Ocean 111
Ayr 127

Baccach, John 150
Balliol, John 146
Balloch, Donald 154, 155, 157
Ban, Donald 8
Bannerman, John 58
Bannockburn, battle of (1314) 150
bards 159–60
Bargarran, battle of 35, 88, 119
Bede, Venerable 36
Ben More 38

Benbecula 138

bi-lingualism 139

birlinns 114–16

Birsay Episcopalian church 48

Black Douglas 149

Blathmac, son of Fland 26

Blood Eagle 6

Bloody Bay, battle of 158

Book of Clanranald, The 64, 160

Book of Islay, The 74, 85

Boraimhe, Brian, High King of Ireland
44

Brandskog rock carvings 97

Bremner, RL, *The Norsemen in Alban*
15, 23, 59

Bretons 34

British army 165

Brøgger, Professor AW 93, 100, 102, 104

Bronze Age boats 97

Bruce, Robert *see* Robert I, the Bruce,
King of Scotland

Bruces 145

Buchanan, George 87

Bute 45, 70, 72, 120, 124, 126

Cadwallader, Prince of Gwynedd 74

Cairbre Riata 36

Caithness 3, 5, 25, 32, 34, 47, 48, 122,
127

Cambrensis, Giraldus 43

Campbel, Gillespic 146

Campbell, Colin, Earl of Argyll 157

Campbell, John 154

Campbell, Sir Colin 146

Campbell, Sir Neil 146, 149, 150, 151

Campbells of Loch Awe 144–6, 149,
150, 151, 165

Canmore, Malcolm *see* Malcolm III,
King of Scotland

Capercaille 141

Carloway 133

Carmen de Morte Sumerlidi 88–9

Carswell, John, Bishop of the Isles 159

carvel technique 114

Castle Sween 32, 46, 66, 67

Castle Urquhart 152

castles 63, 66, 67–8, 148, 161 *see also*
under individual names

cattle epidemic 82

Cellach, Abbot of Iona 25

Celts 15, 18, 139, 141

Cenèl Loairn 58

Chatillon, Baron Hugh de 161

Christianity 29–30, 48 *see also* abbeys;
churches; monasteries

Chronicle of Holyrood, The 12, 76, 82,
84, 86

Chronicle of Man, 15, 16, 41, 80, 83,
87, 93–4, 121, 123, 124

Chronicle of Melrose, The 8, 82

Chronicle of Stephen, The 12

Chronicle of Symeon of Durham, The 21

Chronicles of York, The 13

churches 8, 20, 26, 27–8, 30, 73, 80

Clan Cholla 38, 61, 94, 113, 165

Clan Donald *see* MacDonalds

clan system 65, 122, 164–5

feuds 154–5, 158

Clanranald 114

clinker-built ships 18, 95, 98, 101, 113

Clontarf, battle of (1014) 44

Clyde, Firth of 70

Coll 74, 120

Colla brothers *see* Clan Cholla

Colla Uis 58–9

colonisation 19, 24, 27

Colonsay 74, 150

Columba

church of 30, 73

relics of 26

Columcille monastery, Kells,
County Meath 25

Conaire Moglama, Ard Righ Eireann 36

Conn Cheud Chath, Ard Righ Eireann
36, 56, 58

Council of the Isles 68

County Fermanagh 61

Cowal 38

Cowal and Knapdale 32

Crofters Holdings Act (1886) 138

Crovan, Godred 15, 16, 28, 44, 94
Culloden, battle of (1746) 124, 137
cultural revival 139, 141 *see also* Gaelic
culture and language
Cumbria 41, 86
curraghs 18

Dalriada 43, 56, 163
Dalriadic Scots 13, 14, 22, 36, 55
Danes 14, 15, 41
Danish Hjortspring ship 97
David, Earl of Huntingdon 144
David I, King of Scotland 8, 12, 20–1,
    34, 70–1, 73–4, 75
de Lacy, Hugh 123
Denmark 5
Derry 123
Diarmid 146
Diarmit, Abbot of Iona 26
Dingwall 26
Dingwall Castle 162
Domangart 56
Douglas, Earl of 155
Dragons (warships) 110
Druim Alban, mountains of 5, 13
Dubh, Godfrey 75
Dublin 16, 26
Dublin Norse 43–5, 65, 72, 75, 79
Dugall, King of Man and the Isles 80,
    83
Dugall, son of Somerled 119–21, 123
Dumferline 71
Dunaverty Rock 66
Dunbar, J 152
Duncan, Earl of Fife 82
Dunfermline 9
Dunkeld 25
Dunollie Castle, Lorn 148
Dunstaffnage Castle 149, 150
Duntulm Castle, Skye 113

Edgar, King of Scotland 6
education 138–9, 141
Edward I, King of England 21, 142, 146,
148, 149

Edward II, King of England 149, 150
Edward IV, King of England 157
Elgin 152
England 8–9, 20–1, 44, 121, 122, 142,
    144–6, 157
Eochaidh 38
Eriboll 25
Eric II, King of Norway 142
Ethelred, Prince 12
Eugenius I, King 87
Ewan of Lorn 125–6
Eyrbyggia Saga 27
Eystein, brother of Sigurd 22
Eystein III Haraldsson 22

Falaise, Treaty of (1174) 122
famine 82
farm names 130, 134
Feradach of Strathearn 84
Fergus MacFerdach 36
Fergus Mòr, Lord of Galloway 38, 41,
    72, 74, 79, 84
feudalism 9, 73, 124, 164
Fife 32, 34
Fingal of Man 16
Finlaggan Castle, Islay 68, 70, 162, 163,
    165
Fionnphort 67
Firth of Clyde 70
Firth of Lorn 66
Fitzallan, Walter, High Steward of
Scotland 70
Flaithbertach u-Brolchain 85
Flanders 21, 34
Florence, Count of Holland 85
fort names 133
France 21
Frodi 43

Gaelic culture and language 19, 38, 124,
    129–33, 159–60, 163, 164
Gaels 3, 5, 23, 64, 65
Gàidheil of Argyll 55
Gall-gàidheil people 3, 15, 27, 41, 43,
    44, 55, 65

galleys 94–5, 95, 113–14, 161
Galloway 41–2, 82, 84, 94
Gavelkind 24, 119–20, 123
Gigha 74, 126, 150
Gilleadamnan, grandfather of Somerled
    56, 61
Gillebride, father of Somerled 6, 7, 61,
    110
Gillecolum, son of Somerled 88
Gilli(-brigid), King of Innsigall 59
Glasgow 139
Godred the Black 18, 22, 45, 49, 76,
    79–80, 82, 84, 85, 110
Godrey, son of Fergus MacErc 56, 59
Gofrey Sigtryggsson (MacSitric), King
of Man and the Isles 16, 44
Gokstad ship 98, 99, 100–8, 109, 110,
    111–12
Grant, Dr IF 58
grave ships 109
Great Ships class 110
Greenland 22
Gregorian reform movement 20
Gregory, Donald 56–8, 87, 120
guerrilla warfare 13, 61, 62

Hafrsfiordr, battle of (872) 27, 47
Hakon Hadonssonn, King of Norway
    49, 110
Hakon IV, King of Norway 121, 124–7
Halfdan Longleg 6
Halsenoy ship 97–8
Harald, Earl of Orkney 49
Harald, Earl of the Nordreys 122
Harald Fairhair's Saga 6, 27, 43
Harald Haarfagre (Fairhair),
    King of Norway 7, 16, 26, 27, 47
Harald Hardradi, King of Norway 16
Harald IV Gille, King of Norway 22
Harlaw, battle of (1411) 58, 89, 153
harps 160
headlands 134
Hebrides 3, 16, 19, 24–5, 27, 80, 85,
    114, 124–5, 163
Henry, Duke of Northumberland 82

Henry, Prince 75, 76
Henry I, King of England 8, 20–1, 71,
    73
Henry II, King of England 20, 34, 82,
    84, 85, 86, 121
Henry III, King of England 126
Henry V, Emperor of Germany 21
Hibernia 38
Highland University 141
Highlands 9, 13, 70, 88, 122, 124,
    137–8, 161
Holy Island monastery,
    off Arran 123
Holyrood 9
Hoveden, Roger 87
Hugh, Earl 30
Hugh Anrahan 67
hulls 101–2, 114
Hunter, James 162
Huntley, Earl of 157

Iceland 22, 27
Icelandic Annals 124
Inge I Krokrygg, King of Norway
    22, 76, 79, 80, 82, 85
inheritance
    Gavelkind 24, 119–20, 123
    primogeniture 9, 76, 120, 142
    Tanistry 9, 12, 32, 76, 120
Inner Hebrides 19
Innse-Gall 19, 46, 49, 59, 65, 129
Inverlochy, battle of (1431) 155
Inverness 5, 139
Iona 25, 26, 29–30, 67, 85, 123, 124, 160
Ireland 25, 31, 61, 75, 121
    Dublin Norse 43–5, 65, 72, 75, 79
intermarriages 55–6
    migration to Scotland 36, 38
    Viking raids 26
Iron Age boats 97
iron ore 23, 24
island names 133
Islay 16, 28, 29, 74, 110, 119, 120, 129
    Earl of Ross 157, 158
    Finlaggan Castle 68, 70, 162, 163, 165

Norse influence 133–5
Ivan Beinlaus 15

Jacobite Rebellion (1715) 13
James I, King of Scotland 153, 155
James II, King of Scotland 155
James III, King of Scotland 157
James IV, King of Scotland 160
Jane, daughter of Angus MacSomerled
 123
Jedburgh 9
Jura 74, 120, 150

keels 100–1, 112
Kelso 9
Kenneth MacAlpin, King of Scotland
 3, 9, 14, 22, 25, 55, 56, 58
kerling (crone) 102, 104–5, 107
Kerrera, island of 126
Kerrera, Sound of 66
Ketil Flatnose 15, 16, 24, 27
Kinloss 9
Kintyre 6, 30, 38, 44, 65, 68, 70, 82,
 101, 124, 126, 129, 135–7, 152, 157–8
Knapdale 65, 67, 152, 157
Kvalsund ship 98–9
Kyle of Tongue 25

Lagman (son of Crovan),
 King of the Hebrides 16
Lagmar Lodbrok 15
land
 grants 150
 inheritance 24, 119–20, 123
 settlement 47
Landnámabók 27
language see Gaelic culture and language
Largs, battle of (1263) 127
Leinster 16, 45
Lennox, Earls of 149
Leslie, Mary 153
Lewis, Isle of 16, 28, 94, 126, 129–33
Limerick 15
Lindisfarne, raid on (793) 25
literature 159–60

Livingstone, Sir James 155
Loch Aline 66
Loch Creran 66
Loch Finlaggan 68
Loch Linnhe 66
Loch Lomond 127
Loch Loskin 38
Loch na Keal 67
loch names 133
Lochaber 66, 67
Lock Etive 66
log boats 95, 96
'Long Serpent' 109
longships 23, 24, 26, 46, 62, 80, 83, 89
 coastal 109–10
 evolution of 92–100
 Gokstad 98, 99, 100–8, 109, 110,
  111–12
 size classification system 110–11
 Somerled 88, 94
Lords of the Isles 15, 56, 68, 123, 151,
 152–62
Lorn 65, 66, 71, 120
Louise, Princess 145
Lulach, King 9, 12, 70

MacArthurs 160
MacBain, A 120
MacBeths 9, 12
MacCodrums 160
MacCrimmons 160
MacDonald, Alexander,
 Lord of the Isles 153–5
MacDonald, Angus, great-grandson
 of Somerled 126
MacDonald, Angus Òg 149, 150, 151
MacDonald, Donald, Lord of the Isles
 152–3
MacDonald, Hugh 56, 62, 87, 88, 89,
 120
MacDonald, John,
 Lord of the Isles 152, 154
MacDonald, Rev A and MacDonald,
 Rev A 165–6
MacDonald galley 95, 113

MacDonalds 36, 38, 82, 87, 88, 94, 120, 123, 144, 145, 154–5, 158, 164–5
  ancestry of 53, 55–60
MacDougalls 144, 149, 150, 164–5
MacEacharna, Domhnall 60, 134–5
MacEacherns 161
MacErc, Fergus 56, 59
MacFergus, Godfrey, lord of Oriel 56, 58
MacHeth, Angus, Earl of Moray 12, 20
MacHeth, Donald 82–3
MacHeth, Malcolm, Earl of Ross 12–13, 20, 70, 73–4, 76, 82–3, 85
MacHeths 70, 84
MacInneses of Morven 62
Mackenzie, Kenneth 137
MacKinnons 161
MacLiers 75
MacMhurrichs 160
MacNeill, Maurice 88
MacNeills of Barra 115–16
MacPhees 160–1
MacPoke the hermit 75
MacRuries 164–5
MacSporrans 161
MacSuibhne, Ewan 68
MacTadc, Donald 18
MacVurich the bard 58
MacWilliam, Donald 122
Magnus, King of Norway 5–6
Magnus Bareleg's Saga (Heimskringla) 5, 28–9, 30, 45, 101
Magnus III (Bareleg), King of Norway 16, 22, 27, 28–31, 45
Magnus IV, King of Norway 22
Magnus VI, King of Norway 127
Malcolm I, King of Scotland 5
Malcolm III, King of Scotland 8, 16, 30
Malcolm IV, King of Scotland 34, 75, 82, 84, 85–6, 121
Malsnechtai 12
Man, Isle of 25, 28, 124, 129
Man and the Isles, kingdom of 15–18, 22, 30–1
  alliance with Argyll 71–2
  Dublin Norse 44–5

  Olaf's nephews and 76, 79
  and Scottish Crown 121
  taken back by Godred the Black 79–80
  taken by Somerled 83
  manuscripts 23, 25
Mar and Buchan 32, 34
Margaret, Maid of Norway 142, 144
Margaret, Princess 152
Margaret, Queen of Scotland 8, 9, 73
Margaretsons 9, 73
Martin, Martin 160
martyrdom 26
masts 104–7, 113, 114
Matilda, Empress (daughter of Henry I) 21, 71, 73
Matilda, Queen (sister of David I) 8, 20, 21
media 141
Melrose 9
mercenaries 40
Methven, battle of 148
migration 24, 36
Moidart 66, 68
monasteries 8–9, 20, 25, 26, 123
Moray 3, 5, 9, 12, 13, 32, 34, 65, 152
Moray, Angus MacHeth, Earl of 12, 20
Moray rebellion 20–21, 70
Morven 7, 61, 66, 67, 120
Muirchertach, High King of Ireland 16, 79, 85
Muireadhach Tireach 38
Mull 16, 28, 29, 74, 120
Mull, Isle of 66
Mull, Sound of 66
Munster 36
music 141, 159

Nairn 5
names
  personal 27, 56, 129, 133, 137, 145–6
  place 18, 36, 38, 67, 129–33
Newbattle 9
Nial's Saga 44
Nordreys *see* Orkney; Shetland

Normandy 20, 21
Normans 8, 9, 34, 73, 75, 76, 79, 82,
    84, 146
Norsemen 3, 5, 7, 14, 22
    in Argyll 61, 62, 64–7, 119
    Dublin 43–5, 65, 72, 75, 79
    fractionalised 26
    influence in Scotland 129–41
    Man and the Isles 15, 18
    migration from Ireland to Scotland
        41
    Orkneys 46–9
    plundering expeditions 22–3, 24–6,
        99, 124, 126, 127
    and possible Somerled ancestry
        59–60
North Uist 75
Northern Ireland 159
Northern Isles 46, 47
Northumbria 5, 6, 41, 82, 86, 121, 122
Norway 3, 5
    collusion with Godred the Black 80
    colonisation 23–4, 27
    end of presence in Scotland 125–8
    fragmentation of 22
    Harald Haarfagre's reign 26, 27
    and Ireland 43, 121
    Kintyre 30
    Magnus Bareleg's reign 28–31
    Orkneys and 46–7
    shipbuilding 95–9
    subduing the west coast 124–5
    tribute 15–16, 18, 28, 31, 44
Nydam ship 98

oars 97, 107
oarsmen 104, 110
O'Daly (bard) 160
O'Duihne, Eva 146
Òg, Angus 157, 158
Olaf, brother of Sigurd 22
Olaf Godredsson (Olaf the Red or
Bitling), King of Man and the Isles
    15–18, 31, 41, 45, 60, 71–2, 74–5, 76
Ollamh, office of 160

Orderic Vitalis 12, 20
Orkney 16, 22, 24, 25, 27, 28, 43, 46–9,
    80, 127
Orkneyinga Saga 47
Oronsay 123
Oseberg 'royal yacht' 109
Ospack 124
Ottar Ottarssonn, King of Dublin 75
Ottarsson, Thorfinn 80
Outer Hebrides 19, 22, 49, 129, 161

Paisley 9
Paisley Abbey 123
Pass of Brander, battle of (1309) 149, 150
Perth 84
Perth, Treaty of (1266) 127–8
Picts 3, 13, 14, 22, 23, 25, 43, 48, 55
pipers 160
piracy 24, 44, 45, 47, 49, 94
plague 82
poetry 29, 46
portage 101, 112, 127
primogeniture 9, 76, 120, 142
Prudentius of Troyes 47

Ragnhildis, wife of Somerled 18, 41,
    60, 72
ransom victims 24
Rathlin 25, 43
Reginald, son of Somerled 85, 119–21,
    122–3
Rì 32–5, 73, 74, 76, 82, 84, 88
Riata brothers 36
Rìgh Fhionngall 18
River Shiel 64
Robert, Prince 20
Robert I, the Bruce, King of Scotland
    142, 144, 148–50
Robert II, King of Scotland 152
Robert III, King of Scotland 152
rock carvings 97
Roman Catholic Church 73, 80
Ronald Thorkelssonn, King of Dublin
    75
Ross 5, 65, 122

Ross, Earls of 153 *see also* MacHeth,
    Earl of Ross, Malcolm
Ross, John, Earl of 155, 157–8
Ross & Cromarty 139, 153
Rothesay Castle 124
Roxburgh Castle 12, 74, 82
Royal House of Scotland 140, 142, 150
    see also under individual kings
rudders 99, 105–6, 112, 113
Run Rig 141

Saddell Abbey, Kintyre 85, 89, 123
Scone 25
Scotia 38
Scotland 47, 49, 152–9
Royal House of 140, 142, 150
seannachies 159–60
Shetelig, Hakon 98, 100
Shetland 22, 27, 47, 80
shipbuilding 95–108, 101–2, 112, 113–14,
    137, 161
ships *see* birlinns; galleys; longships
Sigurd, Earl of Orkney 44
Sigurd, King of Man and the Isles 16
Sigurd, King of Norway 22, 48
Sigurd II Munn 22
Sigurd the Stout, Earl of Orkney 59
Sitric, King of Dublin 44
Skene, Dr WF 32, 55, 87, 120
skin boats 95–7
Skipness 68
Skye 16, 25, 28, 49, 74, 75, 120, 126,
    153, 157
slaves 23, 24, 44, 45
Somerled the Mighty 3, 6–7, 21, 45, 61,
    163–4
    alliance with Rì 32, 34
    ancestry 53, 55–60
    capture of Man and the Isles 83
    character and appearance 62
    and David I 70–1
    death of 35, 89, 119
    and Godred the Black 80, 82, 83
    and Iona 85
    Irish support for 38, 40, 65

king of the Sudreys 85
longship fleet 83, 110
and Malcolm IV 75, 76, 86–8
and Malcolm MacHeth, Earl of
    Ross 73–4
marriage 18, 41, 60, 72
and Nordreys 47, 48, 49
and Olaf 18
as resistance leader 62, 64, 65–7
rise of the clan of 145
South Uist 138
Southland 25
sports 161
Stamford Bridge, battle of (1066) 16, 45
Stephen, King of England 20, 72, 73, 82,
    86
Stewarts 145, 150
Stirling, AMW 120
Stirling Castle 150
Stone Age boats 95–7
stone carvings 160
Stornoway 94
strakes 101–2, 107
Strathclyde 44, 139
Strathearn and Mentieth 32, 34
Sudreys 22, 30, 31, 59, 85, 127
Suibhne, son of Hugh Anrahan 32, 67
Sunart 66
Sutherland 3, 5, 47, 48
Sutherland, John Douglas, later ninth
    Duke of Argyll 145
suzerainties 22, 43, 46, 85, 119
Sverre, King of Norway 110, 122
Swein (Viking raider) 26

Tanist Law 9, 12, 32, 76, 120
Tantallon Castle 154, 155
Tarbert 126
Tarbert Castle 148
Taynuilt 38
Teutonic tribes 24
Thomas II, Archbishop of York 13
Thorfinn the Mighty, Earl of Orkney
    48, 59
Thorgils 43

Thorolf, Bishop 48
Tighe, Luchd 161
timber 24, 112, 161
Tioram Castle 66, 68
Tiree 16, 28, 29, 74, 120
torture 6
trade 24, 43–4, 161
Trygvason, Olaf 109
Tune ship 109
Twenty-fives 110

Uists 16, 28
Ullapool 25
Ulster 22, 25
Ulva, island of 67

Vikings *see* Norsemen; Norway
violence 6, 23, 26

Wade, General 13
Wales 30
Wallace, Sir William 148
Western Isles 5, 22, 27, 74, 75, 126–8,
    139, 158
William II, King of England 30
William the Conqueror 16, 146
William the Lion, King of Scotland
    121, 122
Wimund 13